The brilliant young Korean-American novelist who electrified readers with *The Martyred* has now written a deeply moving impression of the Korea he knew as a child during the Japanese occupation. Taking its title from the grim fact that the occupiers forced the Koreans to renounce their own names and adopt Japanese names instead, the book consists of seven vivid scenes drawn from the author's childhood and early adolescence. Each is a self-contained drama, exploring, in some way, the problem of oppression and what happens to a people when their language, their culture, and even their names are taken from them. The question of whether one merely tries to survive or risks one's life in fighting back is a leitmotiv throughout.

Specifically, this is the story of one Korean family, how it endured a prolonged period of national crisis, and how a young boy saw and was shaped by these circumstances. The opening vignette is effectively presented through the eyes of the mother, as she and her young husband make a hazardous crossing into Manchuria by foot across the frozen Tuman River, carrying their infant son. Later episodes take place near Pyongyang, Korea, where the boy experiences injustice and brutality in the Japanese-run school and develops the activist character that is so dramatically demonstrated at the book's conclusion.

Looming large in the boy's field of vision is the strong, beloved father—a respected leader in the Korean resistance, who, when not imprisoned by the Japanese, was at least under close surveillance. With his father's example before him, it is perhaps not a complete surprise that, at one point, the boy responds to an unjust, merciless beating from a Japanese teacher by fighting back, but the raw courage required for such an act *is* startling, and its effect is heightened when the boy further defies the Japanese by sabotaging the school play's tribute to the Emperor.

While the book evokes a poignant sense of a particular people, place, and time—the anguish of the Korean people during World War II—its universal implications remain equally haunting.

Lost Names

Scenes from a Korean Boyhood

RICHARD E. KIM

PRAEGER PUBLISHERS

New York • Washington • London

PRAEGER PUBLISHERS
111 Fourth Avenue, New York, N.Y. 10003, U.S.A.
5, Cromwell Place, London S.W.7, England

Published in the United States of America in 1970
by Praeger Publishers, Inc.

© 1970 by Praeger Publishers, Inc.

Library of Congress Catalog Card Number: 71–83338

Printed in the United States of America

*To my father and mother,
and for my children*

Contents

LOST NAMES

Crossing

". . . and the twilight, yes, the twilight," says my mother, closing her eyes for a moment. "The sun goes down quickly in the north, you know, especially in the winter." She pauses, remembering the twilight and the sunset in a small border town by Tuman River that separates northern Korea, Manchuria, and Siberia. 1933—I must have been only a year old. "Oh, but that twilight was glorious, almost awesome," says my mother. "It was windy that afternoon, and snow flurries were swirling and swishing around all over—over the shabby little town, the snow-covered railway station, the ice-capped mountains, the frozen river, the bridge, yes, the bridge which we had to cross but couldn't. Of course, I didn't see it all really until I was out of the train, until they took your father away from me, away from the train we were on." She stops again, as if to blot out that part of her remembrance —the Japanese Thought Policeman and the Japanese Military Policeman snatching away my father's papers and pushing him down the corridor and out of the train. She shakes her head slightly and smiles. "And it was so cold in the train. The steam heater wasn't working, not in our compartment anyway, and I had only thin socks on." Her thin cotton socks and her black patent leather shoes—and she is the only Korean woman in the compartment who wears Western-style clothes, has a baby, and has to watch, in tearful silence, her young husband being taken off the train by the Japanese.

And what was I doing? Asleep? Awake, wide awake—watching too. "And I almost wished you would start crying, and the Japanese would let your father alone so he could take care of me and you, but you didn't." She smiles. "We had been on the train almost all day, when it, at last, pulled into that railway station. The compartment was half-empty, cold, and there was a thick coat of ice on the windows, and you couldn't see out."

. . . the train gasps and puffs into the outer edge of the train yard, braking hard, slipping on the tracks. "Where are we?" my mother is asking, holding me up in her arms as the train jerks and lurches. "This is the last stop before the border," my father is saying, "this is the last Korean town before we get to Manchuria." Frozen windowpane crusted with sooty ice. My father scratching the pane with his thumbnail, thawing it with his breath, and clearing a round patch with his fingers, so my mother and I can look outside, so his young wife can look at the last town on the Korean side of the border, before they take leave of their homeland that is no longer their homeland. She watches the snow flurries whipping and gyrating madly outside, subsiding suddenly once in a while, and she can see nothing for a while, as the train crawls into the station. Then, the train is slinking in between other trains and flatcars, and she is staring at the big guns of the Japanese artillery and the tanks on the flatcars and, then, the horses of the Japanese cavalry peering out of their open stalls next to the flatcars, the horses' white breath mixing with the steam from the train, and, then, the Japanese soldiers in their compartments, all looking out, some in their undershirts and some with their jackets open, eating and drinking. She turns to my father and says:

"Look."

My father looks out, turns to her, and nods.

It is then that a Japanese Thought Police detective and a Japanese Military Policeman come into the compartment. The detective is a middle-aged Korean who works for the Japanese; he is big and tall and wears a brown, dog-fur coat and a gray felt hat. The Japanese Military Policeman is not wearing an overcoat; he has on a brown leather belt with a big brass buckle, a pistol in a black leather holster, and a long saber that his white-gloved left hand clutches; he is young and short, with a flushed, boyish face; he is a corporal. "There were only about a dozen people in our compartment," says my mother, "and the detective took one look around and came straight to your father. He knew what he was up to. The Military Policeman followed right behind him, like a hunter following behind his hound, and all the Korean passengers were looking at us, all very quiet. When the detective came to our seat, he turned around to look at the other passengers, and they all snapped their heads away from us, and the detective nodded to the Japanese Military Policeman." She stops. "As if to say to the corporal, 'Well, we got him.' "

. . . and she is looking down at the snow-covered toes of the corporal's long, brown boots and the shiny toes of the detective's black shoes. The thin fingers of her young husband smoothing pieces of creased papers and holding them out, and the white-gloved hand of the corporal snatching them up. The papers crackle, and she thinks her husband's hand is trembling, not because he is afraid but because he is in poor health and weak; after all, he had been jailed by the Japanese for years for his resistance-movement activities, before she married him. . . . The corporal gives the papers to the detective and steps aside. His boots creak, and, as if on cue, the Korean detective says to her husband—my father—"So, you don't waste much time, do you? You could hardly wait to get out of the country."

My father is silent.

"Your parole was over only a week ago, and here you are sneaking out of the country."

"My papers are in order, as you can see," says my father, "and you must have had words about me from the police in my town."

"We know everything about you."

"Then you know I have official permission to travel."

"A piece of paper," says the detective.

"It is signed by the chief of police in my town and also by the Japanese judge of our district."

The detective folds the papers and stuffs them into his pocket. "What is the purpose of your travel?"

"It is stated in the papers."

"I am asking you a question."

"I have a job waiting for me."

"You couldn't get a job in the country?"

"I was a farmer," says my father. "I worked in my father's orchard."

"So—this high school is run by foreign missionaries. Do you have to work for foreigners?"

My mother thinks my father should say, "Look, you, too, are working for foreigners, as their hound." But my father says quietly, "It's a job."

"These missionaries—these foreign Christians—they feel sorry for you and give you a job and think they are protecting you from us?"

"It's a job; besides, I am a Christian," my father says and quickly glances at my mother. "And my wife is the daughter of a Christian minister, so it is natural that the foreign missionaries would want to hire me to teach."

"What do they want you to teach?"

"I am going to be teaching biology and chemistry."

The detective doesn't reply to that and looks at my mother.

My father says, "She will be teaching music at the school's kindergarten. It is all stated in the papers."

The detective says to my mother, "Is that a boy or a girl?"

I am all bundled up and wrapped in the wool blanket my grandmother made.

"A boy," says my mother. "He is only a year old."

My father says, "May I have the papers back?"

The detective says, "Do you understand Japanese?"

My father nods. "I don't speak it well."

The detective whispers something to the Japanese corporal. He turns to my father. "You must come with us."

"Why?"

"The Military Police want to ask you a few questions."

"About what?"

"How would I know! I don't work for the Military Police!"

"But I can't leave the train. It will go out soon."

"No, it won't move for a while. The military trains will have to cross the bridge first, and that will take a while. Come!" He says to my mother, "You stay here. He will be back soon."

She tries to stand up, gathering me up in her arms. My father tells her not to worry. "Stay here," he says. Tears well up in her frightened eyes, and her husband shakes his head. She nods and sits down, clutching me close to her. He moves out of the seat, and she picks up his woolen gloves and hands them to him. Then, they are gone from the compartment. She presses her face to the window, trying to see if she can catch a glimpse of him, trying to find out where they are taking him. But all that she can see is the Japanese military train that is right alongside her train. The military train is now creaking out of the station and, through the frozen windowpane, she sees blurred images of the Japanese guns, tanks, soldiers, and the horses that are passing by. At last, she can see across the snow-covered tracks to the dingy station house, just as my father and his inquisitors disappear into it. Her breath is clouding the windowpane, and a thin coat of ice quickly blots out her view. Scratching at the windowpane, she is trying to be brave, but she is afraid for her young husband and for herself, alone with the baby; she weeps silently, all the time thinking that she must do something. It is quiet in the compartment; the other passengers try not to look at her. A little later, the conductor comes in and begins to collect the tickets. She doesn't have her ticket; her husband has it. She looks up at the conductor, who is a Korean, and tries to explain but words do not come out. A young Korean boy, a high school boy, comes over and quickly explains the situation to the conductor, who nods in sympathy and tells her not to worry. The high school boy bows to her and shyly asks her the name of her husband. She tells him. The boy smiles triumphantly, knowingly.

"I heard his name mentioned by the detective, but I wanted to make sure," he says, glancing at the conductor, who is standing by awkwardly. The boy says to her, "I go to the same high school he went to in Seoul. Everyone at the school knows his name and about his trial and going to prison and all." He tells the conductor that my father is a patriot who, as a college student, organized a resistance movement against the Japanese and was arrested by the Japanese and spent years in prison. He tells the conductor the name of the trial case. The conductor says he has heard about it and turns to her. "He will be all right. Don't worry too much. It probably is just a routine questioning. This is a border town, you know, and, what with the war and all the disturbances going on across the river—well, the Japanese have been pretty strict about security."

The high school boy whispers, "Is it true that the Chinese and Korean troops across the river demolished a whole Japanese regiment a while ago?"

The conductor hushes the young boy but nods. "In June," he says. "The regiment from Nanam." He cuts the cold air with his gloved hand. "All of them." He says to the boy, "I would be quiet about it, though, if I were you."

"Yes, sir," says the boy.

Suddenly, the train lurches forward and begins to move.

The conductor says, "What's going on? We aren't supposed to pull out for another hour!" He runs out of the compartment, saying, "I'll find out and let you know."

My mother, in panic, stands up, swaying. Quickly, she makes up her mind that she should get off the train. She gathers me up in her arms but doesn't know what to do with the two suitcases. The train slows down and stops. The boy says, "You can't get off the train! They wouldn't let the train go out without him. Trains can't go out without the Military Police's permission, you know."

But she is now determined. She should have followed her husband, she thinks, when they took him away. She is afraid, and she feels lost. She says to the boy, "I am going out."

The boy says, "The train is stopped now. Why don't you wait and see?"

The conductor runs into the compartment and shouts to everyone, "We'll be moving out in a minute!" He comes to her. "What are you going to do?"

"She wants to get off the train," says the boy.

"No, no! You mustn't!" says the conductor. "Look! I can tell the station clerk about your husband and have him tell your husband that you will be waiting for him across the river. He can join you there. There's another train coming in about two hours."

"That's a good idea," says the boy. "You can come with me and my mother and stay with us. We live right across the river. We can leave our address with the station clerk."

She doesn't answer. She quickly wraps me up tightly and is out of her seat.

The conductor says, "If you insist, then I'll take you to the station clerk who is a friend of mine. A Korean. It will be warm in his office, and you can wait there. Come."

She says to the boy, "Would you do me a favor? Would

you mind taking these suitcases with you and leaving them at the station across the river?"

The conductor says, "I'll help him. We can leave them with the Chinese station master there."

She thanks them all and starts down the corridor.

Someone says, "Take care of yourself."

Outside, icy wind and snow flurries lash at her. Her shoes are quickly buried under the snow on the tracks. She covers my face with the blanket, trudging across the tracks toward the station house. The conductor is carrying a small bag for her. Before they clear the tracks and climb up an embankment, the train they just left clanks and begins to move. The conductor, helping her up the embankment, swears under his breath. "I can't come with you. I must run back to the train. Be careful now and tell the station clerk I sent you. I may see you both on the other side of the river." He leaps over the tracks and runs back to the moving train. Her words of thanks are lost in the wind. She is now standing on the platform, which is deserted, except for a Japanese Military Policeman who is flagging the train out. She looks at the train chugging out of the yard, and she can see the old conductor and the young boy standing on the step of the compartment she was in. They are waving to her. Tears run down her frozen cheeks, and she silently watches the train move across the bridge, across the river, toward Manchuria. She hugs me close and wipes away her cold tears, rubbing her face against the blanket that keeps me warm. She looks up, aware that the Japanese Military Policeman is watching her, and it is then that she, standing forlorn on the barren platform, sees that it is twilight.

The sun, big and red in spite of the snow flurries, is setting, plummeting down toward the frozen expanse of the northern Manchurian plains. "Twilight"—she thinks—"it is twilight," and, somehow, she forgets everything for a moment, lost in the awesome sight of the giant, red sun, which, as though burning out, is swiftly sinking and being swallowed up by the darkening northern horizon. The silvery snow flurries are dancing in the air, whishing and roaring, as if cleansing the lingering rays of the bloody sun from the northern sky. . . . The air is cool and fresh, and she prays, "Lord, help me."

The sun has disappeared. It is now dark. The wind has died down. My mother is still standing there alone on the platform. I am asleep in her arms. She is facing toward the bridge. She can't see it clearly now. Only the red lights on both sides of its entrance and its dim silhouette against the starry northern sky are visible. Occasionally, she looks back at the main door of the station house. She can see a small room to the right of the station house; it is lighted inside by a green-shaded lamp that dangles from the ceiling. Someone inside the room, hunched over a little potbellied stove, gets up once in a while and looks out the window. My father is somewhere in town at the Japanese Military Police Detachment. "Too far to walk," said a Korean man, a ticket clerk at the station. "Why don't you and the baby come inside and keep warm?" My mother said no—she would wait for her husband outside; he might come any moment. She waits.

How long did she stand there alone waiting for my father? An hour? Two hours? She doesn't know. She only knows that it is getting darker and darker and, now, she can't see even the silhouette of the bridge. Her feet, protected only by the thin cotton socks, are numb, and, without realizing it, she is rocking back and forth. I am now awake and begin to whimper; I am thirsty and hungry. My mother begins to pace, rocking me; she is weeping quietly, swallowing a big lump of irrepressible terror. She says to herself she can't cry, she mustn't cry, and she must be brave. Her father has been in jail, too, on and off, many times because he would say in his sermons things that the Japanese Thought Police did not like; and, of course, her husband. . . .

All the men she knows—her father, husband, brothers-in-

law, and many of her friends' relatives—they have all been to
jail at least once. It was bad last year, she thinks, especially in
May. A lot of Korean men were arrested and interrogated,
and many have not yet returned home; all this began right
after what happened in Shanghai—a Korean patriot threw
bombs and killed the Japanese general who commanded all
the Japanese forces in China, along with several other
Japanese officials; the general and the officials were at a park
in Shanghai, celebrating the birthday of their Sun-God
Emperor. She remembers a Japanese Thought Police inspector who came to her father after that incident; the inspector told him that it would be in the best interest of
everyone in his parish if, in his Sunday sermon, he would
condemn the violent acts committed by a fellow Korean, a
terrorist. Her father would not cooperate, and, the next
day, they came for him and took him away; they released
him two days later, just before Sunday. Her father had been
beaten by the Police; all that he said in his sermon on Sunday
was that God said vengeance was His. The Japanese are
stupid, she thinks; they think the parishioners would believe
their minister if he said what the police forced him to say,
as if people are so stupid and naïve, as if forcing a man to say
what they want him to say would change his soul. . . .

The old ticket clerk opens the window and asks my mother
to come into the room—the baby must be cold. She doesn't
listen to him. Remembering her father and thinking about
him have made her brave and proud. I come from a family
. . . and I am married to a man . . . She lifts her face and
looks at the star-studded night sky, proud; if her father and
her husband can endure the torture and humiliation in-
flicted by the Japanese, she and the baby will endure the cold
wind and the darkness. She lowers her gaze toward the plains
of Manchuria across the river.

Across the river—she thinks—across the river . . . She
almost says to herself that life would be different across the
river, that the family would be away from the Japanese,

and that there would be quiet and peace. . . . Then, she remembers the Japanese guns, tanks, soldiers, horses. . . . The Japanese had conquered Manchuria and set up a puppet regime, just a year before, and they have already begun their invasion of the Chinese mainland itself. All those guns and tanks and soldiers, on their way to China. There are too many Japanese around; the Japanese are everywhere, toting guns and rattling sabers. Staring hard toward Manchuria, she feels neither despair nor sorrow but the outrage of a wounded soul. "Vengeance is Mine." "Lord," she prays, "free us from them and free us from this nightmare." The wind is quiet now, and there is a strange warmth in the air. Her tears flow freely now, but she does not mind. There is only her Lord to see her tears—and now her young husband, who is coming toward her, crossing the yellow patch of light on the snow outside the room.

She stands still and realizes she is crying. She quickly buries her face in the woolen blanket that is keeping me warm, as if to see whether I am awake or asleep, and rubs her tears dry. She suddenly feels that her throat is parched and that she is a little dizzy. She is afraid she may start crying again. She sways and I squirm and whimper, and that steadies her. My father is by her side now, without a word. She thinks he is trembling. He looks at her quietly, and she can see tears in his eyes. She feels her eyes welling up with tears and quickly she hands me to him as if saying, "Here, he is safe." My father takes me in his arms. My mother opens the blanket so that he can see my face. He touches her on the shoulder. She moves a little closer to him and sees that one of his nostrils is stuffed with tissue paper or cotton that is darkened. Then, she sees several welts on his left cheek. A sharp ache needles her heart. He raises one hand and brushes off snowflakes from her hair.

"We missed the train," he says.

"Another train was supposed to come in but it hasn't yet."

"You must be hungry," he says. "I have something for us to eat. Something for the baby, too."

"I am not hungry."

The ticket clerk opens the window and calls out to them. "Come inside! You'll freeze to death. Come!"

My father says, "Let's go inside. He is heating up some rice cakes I brought from the town. Come."

She nods and picks up her small bag. Snowflakes slide off the bag. "The baby can have some powdered milk. Some biscuits."

They walk into the station house. The ticket clerk opens the door to his room and beckons them in. The warm, steamy air makes her feel dizzy again.

"Come in, come in," says the clerk. "Warm yourselves at the stove."

My father says to my mother, "Better sit down away from the stove. It is not good to get too hot all of a sudden, especially when you have been outside so long." He thanks the clerk for inviting them in.

"The least I can do for you young people," says the clerk. "I'll get you some tea. You must be starving. How is the baby doing?"

I am halfway out of the bundle of blankets, sitting up on my mother's lap.

My mother just looks at me, saying nothing.

The clerk says to my father, "Your wife is a strong-willed woman. She just wouldn't come in until you came back." He is heating the rice cakes on a grill placed on the top of the stove.

My father pours tea from an iron kettle into a small china cup and hands it to my mother, who says he should drink it first. He takes a sip and gives the cup to her. He picks me up from my mother and, bending down, notices that her shoes and socks are wet. "Better take your shoes off and dry them," he says.

The clerk, putting the cakes on a piece of cardboard, says,

"Better dry your socks, too, and don't mind me at all."

She takes off her shoes and, turning away from the clerk, removes her wet socks. My father hands her his handkerchief so she can dry her feet. It is stained with blood. She looks up at him and sees the cotton in his nostril. She begins to sob.

"It is all right," he says. "Dry your feet."

The clerk puts a wooden chair between my parents' chairs and puts the cakes down on it. He quietly goes out of the room.

When the clerk returns to the room, my father thanks him and says that they are ready to leave.

The clerk says, "There is another train sometime tonight. Why don't you wait for it here?"

"It may not come," says my father. "It is already several hours late."

"If it doesn't come in, you can stay in town and leave in the morning."

"We'd better go now," says my father. "We can't stay in this town."

"With the baby, on a night like this?"

"We'll be all right."

"I want to go across the river," says my mother, wrapping me up with the blankets.

"We have someone waiting for us across the river," says my father. "Thank you for everything."

"I understand," says the clerk. "Do you know the way?"

My father nods. "I asked some people in town."

"You've got to go downstream a bit. There are always some people coming and going. You'll see them."

They are going to walk across the frozen river. People who can't afford the train have made a footpath across the river.

"There'll be a policeman out there, you know," says the clerk.

"I have my papers," says my father.

By now, my mother has put another pair of thin cotton socks on under the other pair. Her shoes are still damp. I am in my father's arms. She picks up the small bag, ready to go.

The old man says, "Take care of yourself. Raise the baby well." He wraps the leftover rice cakes in a piece of newspaper and puts them into my mother's small bag. He comes over to my father and pats me on the head before my father covers me up with the blanket. My mother unfolds the edge of the blanket carefully so that I will have a small opening to breathe through.

The old man opens the door for them, and my mother bows to him and bids him farewell. My father bows, too. The old man taps him on the shoulder. "Take care of your family," he says.

*   *   *

Half an hour later, they reach the bank of the river. There is a small hut, lighted inside. Smoke is curling up out of a stove pipe through the roof, and sparks fly off into the dark night air. A dozen people are lined up outside the hut to show their papers to a young Korean policeman. Another policeman is inside the hut. My father shows his papers. The policeman nods and waves my parents by. They are behind an elderly couple, and they follow the old people down the bank toward a path through the snow on the frozen river. They can see lights flickering at the other side of the river, on the Manchurian side. It doesn't seem too far. The old man looks back and says to my mother, "The baby must be cold."

She does not answer. I am warm and secure within the wool blankets. My father says to him, "Is the ice thick enough?"

"Nothing to worry about," he says, helping the old woman down the bank. "We've done this many times. Our son lives across the river, you know. You just follow us."

My father stretches out his hand, which my mother takes as she steps onto the ice. It is the first time they have touched hands since they left home, my grandparents' house. "Do you feel all right?" asks my father. She nods.

She goes behind him. Many people are behind her. No one is talking much. The path has been made by lots of footsteps that packed the snow hard. It is jagged and slippery, and my mother's leather shoes do not help her much. Other people are wearing straw shoes and heavy socks, thickly padded with cotton. "If I had a pair of socks like them," she thinks, "I would take off my shoes and walk on in my socks." Someone slips and falls down behind her. My mother stops.

My father stops, too, and asks her if she is all right. They both watch the people helping a young girl up. They look toward the south side of the river, the Korean side, but they can't see anything. With all the snow under the starry sky, the air is stangely white. People move on like ghosts, silently, except for their feet crunching on the ice. "People without a country"—my mother thinks—"people ousted and uprooted from their homeland. Forced out of their land and their homes by the Japanese, who are buying up land cheaply by threat and coercion. Displaced peasants driven out of their ancestral land to find new roots in an alien land." What fate is waiting for these people across the river? What destiny will unfold for her and her family across the river? She gazes at her husband's back. She can't see the baby. She slips on a large chunk of ice and almost falls. In that second, she lost sight of him and the baby and now she wants desperately to be at their side. She wants to touch him and the baby. She hurries over to them.

My father turns around. "Be careful," he whispers. "Here. Hold onto my hand." She is out of breath and clings to his outstretched hand. She opens the blanket a little to look at me. "He is all right. Asleep," says my father. "Poor thing," she says. "Come," he says, "it won't be long." They are halfway across the river.

Later, the old man ahead of them turns around and says, "You have to be careful now. The ice gets thin around here, and there are holes here and there. Last time I came by, I saw some Chinese fishing through holes." The old man squats down and unwraps a bundle he has been carrying on his back. He takes out a kerosene lantern and tries to light it. The wind blows out his match. The old woman tries to help him by crouching next to him and holding her skirt around the lantern, which the old man lights. "You people stay close behind us. Don't worry."

They can see lights and a few huts along the bank. My mother thinks they are now close to the bank, but there is still a long way to go. Then, she thinks of the holes and the thin ice. She clutches my father's hand. The old man's lantern bobs up and down, its yellowish light flickering. "There's a big crack on the left. Be careful," says the old man, holding the lantern high, waving it. Thin ice, holes, a big crack in the ice. She is afraid. "Be careful, dear," she says to her husband.

"We are almost there," he says. "Almost there now."

Almost there. Across the river. She looks toward the bank. There are people standing on the bank. She can see them dimly against the light from the huts. Almost there. Then, it strikes her that there hasn't been anyone going the other way across the river, toward the Korean side. She can hear voices coming from the bank. The sky is clear, and the stars in the northern plains seem larger and brighter than those in other directions. The snow all around her seems so white and almost shining. Her feet are cold and ache, but the crossing is almost over, and she is thinking only that, across the river, someone is waiting for them, someone from the missionary school. She hopes he has brought a buggy with two horses, which, she has heard, people ride in in Manchuria. "Taking a buggy ride in the snow would be nice," she thinks, "just as they do in Russia," or so she has read. Almost there. There will be quarters for them in the town where the school is. Two rooms and a kitchen. Her husband will be a teacher; students will visit them, and, of course, so will his fellow teachers and the missionary people. She, too, will be teaching, at the school's kindergarten. Twenty-five children—so they have written her. Mostly Korean children, but some Chinese and American and Canadian children, too. Almost there, across the river. "Oh—the suitcases," she thinks, "I hope the young boy and the train conductor made sure the suitcases were left with the Chinese station master. Some wool in one of the suitcases. I will knit a wool sweater for him so he can wear it under his coat when he goes to the school to teach, and the baby could use another wool jacket, and maybe another wool cap. Almost there now." "Is the baby still sleeping?" she asks her husband. "Yes," he says. "Just a little more and we'll be there."

The old man's lantern, the lights along the bank like haloes, and the voices calling to them. Almost there now. Then, she is suddenly seized with a violent fear of that strange alien land waiting for her. All those Chinese people there. "The town is almost a Korean town, really," her husband has said to her, "and the school, of course, is for Korean students. It really is like any other Korean town, except that there are lots of Chinese people around you." "A Korean ghetto, that's what it is," she thinks. She has heard from her father that, in many places in Europe, the Jewish people lived together among foreigners who did not welcome them, and the places where they lived were called ghettos. "Like our parish," he said; "We Christians in this country live close to each other around our churches, and that is not much different from the Jewish people living in their ghettos." "Will those Chinese people be friendly?" she wants to ask her husband, but it is not the time to ask a question like that. Almost there. And, suddenly, she again thinks of holes and thin ice and big cracks in the ice. Thin ice, holes, cracks. . . . The bank looms ahead of them, and it is as if, with one big leap over the ice, they can get onto it. But, now that they are so close to the other side of the river, she feels as if she is losing all her will and strength. "We have made it across," she says to herself. And again—holes, cracks, and thin ice frighten her. Thin ice especially. For one moment, she has a blinding vision of crashing through thin ice and being sucked into the cold water and pushed down under the ice . . . one of her hands is clinging to the edge of the ice, but her body is being pulled down and down . . . and the water freezes her instantly and she can't even scream for help but, then, her husband pulls her up out of the water onto the ice and she gets up . . . and asks, "Is the baby still asleep?"

He says, "Yes."

She says to him, squeezing his hand, "We've made it, haven't we?"

"We've made it across," he says, looking straight ahead.

"Good thing the baby slept through."

He turns to her. "Actually, he's been wide awake. All the way."

She smiles. "What a good little boy he is," she says. She is not thinking of thin ice, holes, and big cracks in the ice any longer. After this, she thinks, I can go with my family anywhere, anytime, to the end of the earth. . . .

*   *   *

And so, I, too, crossed that frozen river wide awake, and, years and years later, whenever I think of that crossing, I think of thin ice, holes and big cracks in the ice—especially the thin ice.

"But, I don't think I can do anything like that again," says my mother. "Not any more. I was young then. Lots of people never made it across that river, you know. Drowned or frozen to death when they were caught in a sudden snow-storm. No, I could not do anything like that again."

"But you can and you will," I say to her. "And you have, many times since, if not crossing a frozen river on foot."

She thinks it over. "Well, so I have, haven't I?" She thinks of the thirty some years since the night we crossed the frozen Tuman River. "And you have, too," she says, "on your own, by yourself."

"I have done it many times."

"Well, you've made it across," she says.

And I am still thinking of the thin ice of that frozen river in the north.

Homecoming

It is my first day at the new school. I am going to be in the second grade, although the principal, who is Japanese, at first insisted that I be put in the first grade, so that I could "start everything new and fresh," meaning that whatever education I have had at the missionary-run school in the town in Manchuria ought to be discredited. We returned from Manchuria about a week before, because—as my mother told me when I was helping her pack our things—my father, as the eldest son of his family, ought to come "home" and help his father manage the household and take care of the family's apple orchard and farming and so forth.

"I knew the Japanese would try to make your life difficult," my grandfather says to my father at dinner, "but it pains me to realize they would be so malicious as to make the boy's life miserable, too."

"Fortunately, the assistant principal is an alumnus of my high school in Seoul," my father says, "and he tried to be helpful and persuaded the principal to let the boy take a special examination to see if he can qualify for the second grade. The boy will pass the test."

And, the next day, I pass the examination.

My grandfather is beaming that evening and allows me to have dinner at the same table with him and gives me five large coins wrapped in rice paper. "If you are at all like your father, you should have a good brain," he says, downing rice wine from a small cup that my father fills for him. He passes the cup to my father and fills it for him. My father drinks the wine, holding the cup in both hands. It is unusual for a father to fill the cup he drinks from with wine for his son. My grandfather is expansive that evening. He drinks much wine. "Your father was first in his class in his grade school; third in his high school," he says, turning to my father, "and he would have done well in college, too, except for the . . ." He takes a big swallow of the wine and says to my father, rather abruptly, "Well, does the boy know?"

"I haven't told him."

"Well, you should. A boy his age ought to know what his father is really like."

"He is too young. Someday. Time will come."

My grandfather shakes his head. His silvery white hair glistens in the light. "Yes, yes. Time will come." With his large eyes, he looks fully at my face. "Just remember, your father is someone who has done things which you will be proud of someday."

My father is quiet. He simply pats my head.

"And remember," my grandfather says, "you must do well; you must do better than the Japanese at the school."

"He will do all right," says my father, putting his arm around my shoulders. "He will be all right."

"The Japanese can insult you and humiliate you," says my grandfather, "but they can't take your brain away."

I am speechless. I do not understand what they are saying. Besides, my grandfather's voice is becoming louder and his face redder. "Eat, eat!" he says to me. "You must be strong and healthy to be a man and to be able to walk down the

street with your head high. And don't ever cry just because
some Japanese are mean to you, hear!"

*   *   *

So this is my first day at the new school. My grandfather
and my father have already finished their breakfast and are
getting ready to go out to the apple orchard, which is
about ten miles from the town. Early in the morning, my
grandfather and my father have breakfast together; then,
my grandfather rides out on an oxcart with one of our tenant farmers, who lives alone in small quarters apart from
our house. My father will follow him a little later on his
bicycle.

This morning, my father wants to see me off to school.
He will not, however, come to the school with me. My
mother is going to come all the way to the school. "Just
this morning," says my father. He is wearing a brown hunting cap and a white shirt with the sleeves rolled up. His
face is deeply tanned, and I see the muscles in his arms ripple
as he pumps air into the bicycle tires. My mother leaves
my sister, who is four years younger than I am, with a
maid. The young maid says, "Have a good school day,
Master." I am not used to being called "Master"; in Manchuria, we never had a maid. My mother is wearing a pale
blue dress with a long, billowing skirt and white rubber shoes.
Her hair, combed neatly into a small bun in the back, is
shiny black, and I smell the hair oil, which has the smell of
almond. My father touches my sister on the cheek as she is
carried by the maid. He sets out ahead of us. My mother
and I follow him out of the east gate. I am wearing the
school uniform—a black jacket with a stiff hooked collar
and lots of shiny brass buttons down the front, a pair of
white trousers, and a black cap with the school insignia,
which is a design with cherry blossoms. I am carrying a
small, brown book bag, brand new, a present from my two
uncles who are away in Tokyo, going to college.

The three of us, my father pushing the bicycle, walk down a narrow dirt road. My shiny, new leather shoes get dirty in no time. It is early summer, hot and humid, with the sun already strong. The road is lined with poplars, and there are few houses, until, downhill, we come to a small square where there is a communal well. The well is covered with a large, pentagonal, wooden roof and has a cement base. Small children are out already, getting cool, splashing water at each other. Women are lined up with pails and buckets, and a few of them are doing their wash. When we walk by the well, the women turn to us and bow to my father. My father nods his head, greeting them, and my mother bows back to the women. An old woman wants to "take a good look" at me. She pats me on the head. "She is one of our neighbors," says my father. She has known my father as a child. "Well, you study hard," she says, bending down to bring her face level with mine. I see her small eyes and wrinkles and shriveled mouth. "You must try to be smarter than those Japanese boys." She stretches up and says to my father, "If any of our boys can be smarter than the Japanese brats, it's got to be your son." "He will be all right," he says. My mother says we should hurry. The children are openly staring at me—I am the new boy in the neighborhood.

We move on and we are at an intersection when my father says he must go now and catch up with my grandfather. I bow to him and wish him a good day. We stand there for a minute and watch him ride down the main road.

A boy who is bigger and looks older than I appears from a small house with a thatched roof. The house is shabby, and it has a small wooden door in the middle of a mud wall. The boy is wearing the school uniform, too. He is carrying an old, ragged bag. He stands outside the door and looks me up and down, putting his cap on. There is a large tree by the door, and a rope swing hangs down from a thick branch. He puts his bag down on the ground and sits on the swing, tying the laces on his dirty white sneakers. "You'd better run, or else you're going to be late!" a woman's voice shouts from within the house. The boy does not answer.

My mother walks on, and I say to her, "That boy is going to the same school." She nods. The boy is following us. We walk down the road toward a large plaza, which is a market place on weekends. On the left of the dirt road, there are small shops—a candy store, a butcher shop, a tailor, a pharmacy, a Chinese restaurant, a Chinese laundry, a rice merchant's store, and so forth. I look back and see that the boy is still following us. In front of the pharmacy, my mother is greeted by a middle-aged woman in a gray dress; they chat a while. I stand by idly, sneaking a glance toward the boy, who is now a few paces behind us, squatting down, again tying his shoe laces. He looks at me sideways and makes faces at me, sticking his tongue out. I try to ignore him, but, from the corner of my eye, I am watching him going off toward a hill. Beyond the hill is the school, and I can see hundreds of children streaming up the steep hill toward the main gate of the school. My mother introduces me to the woman. I bow to her without a word and get another pat on the head.

We move on. I am the only one with a parent. All the children are staring at me, whispering with each other. They all seem to know who I am. I hear a boy saying to his friends, five or six of them, that I am the new boy in town, the one who has come back from Manchuria. One of them says, "All dressed up—he must be new at the school." The path up the hill is flanked by rows of acacias. The leaves are dusty and lifeless. The little huts and dingy houses on both sides of the path are dusty, too, and shabby. Thatched roofs of rotting straw, sooty paper windows, and mud walls —poor people live there. Well-to-do people have houses with tile roofs; our house has a tile roof. The children's voices are loud and shrill. We are like an island, surrounded on all sides by the children. At the main gate, all of a sudden, the first boy I saw reappears out of nowhere and sticks his

tongue out at me again. Other children who see it laugh,
squealing and shouting. The boy runs off. Girls, in white and
blue sailor shirts and white skirts, set apart from the boys,
walk by us, staring at me, some giggling, covering their
mouths with their hands. My mother, when we are by the
main gate, says that I am now on my own and asks me if
I think I can find my way back home after school. I nod
quickly, anxious to be left alone, though I am a little afraid
of so many children. The school in Manchuria was small
and had only thirty or forty children. This school must
have several hundred children. I say good-by to my mother,
without looking up at her, and run away, swinging my bag,
not really knowing which building I am supposed to head
for. I look back and cannot see my mother. She has gone.

There is a large, circular flower bed, with a flag pole in
the middle, in front of a big building. The flag—the Japanese flag—is white, with a big red circle in the middle.
There is no breeze in the morning air under the cloudless,
blue sky, and the large flag hangs limp. I stand by the flag
pole, not knowing what to do. In front of me is a large field,
which is now filling up with the children. They are all lining up in formation, class by class, I think; each group has
someone in front who is barking out orders, calling out
names. From another building, to the left, teachers are
emerging. I see a small platform, and a teacher gets up
there, and other teachers are spreading out in front of
the children, who are all facing them. All the male teachers
are wearing identical clothes—khaki jackets and trousers
of the same design as the boys' uniform, which is really
identical, in its turn, to the Japanese military uniform.

The girls, on one side, and the boys, on the other, nearly
fill the large field. All I can see are the boys' black caps and
black jackets and the girls' white and blue sailor shirts and
white skirts. I am still standing by the flag pole, clutching at
my book bag, not knowing what to do with myself. All the
children seem to form groups according to their classes,

with the bigger children, boys and girls, standing in the center of the entire formation. I decide that the first-graders must be the ones standing at the edge of the formation, mainly because these are the littlest ones; so I make up my mind to go to what I think is the group of the second-graders, when a big boy comes over to me. He is wearing a white armband on his left sleeve and insignia on his collar that indicate he is a sixth-grader.

"Are you the new boy?" he says. "The assistant principal said I should look out for a new boy this morning."

I nod silently. His uniform is neat and clean; his trousers are sharply pressed and he is wearing big leather boots with lots of eyelets for laces. His armband says that he is the Student of the Day.

"You are going to be in the second grade, right?"

"Yes, sir." I was told to "sir" the senior students as well as, of course, the teachers.

"Come with me, then," he says, nodding approvingly after looking me up and down. "You look fine. Come on. I'll take you to your class."

I follow him. When we reach the line of the teachers, he stops in front of a teacher and salutes him in a military manner. I see the teacher glance at me and nod. Everyone is looking at me—I think. The boy again salutes the teacher smartly and, holding me by my left arm, takes me around the entire formation, going behind it, and deposits me in the rear of a group of children who must be the second-graders. A small boy who wears a blue armband salutes the big boy with the white armband, and the big boy says to him, "Here. This is the new boy in your class. Look after him."

"Yes, sir," says the small boy. He says to me, after the big boy has gone, "Today, you can stand here in the back. We will figure out where you are going to stand from to-morrow on. I am the class leader." He leaves me and marches back to where he was—in front of the group. I find myself standing next to a small boy, who doesn't look at me at all.

I steal a glance at him. He is rubbing his eyes as if he has just been awakened. His uniform is rather dirty, and he smells bad—sour and sweaty, as if he hasn't bathed for days. Suddenly, I see the boy who followed me and my mother to the school. He is three rows ahead of me. He looks back at me and thumbs his nose, showing his gappy, stained teeth. He has two buck teeth. I look away, feeling a little annoyed and also surprised to learn that he is a second-grader, too, although he is bigger than any of the other children in the group. I don't look at him, but I can hear him grunting like a pig and then oink-oinking. Some children giggle. The class leader trots back to where the big boy is and says sharply, "Shut up!" When the class leader resumes his position, the boy makes noises again, this time pretending he is a tiger—"Grrrrr!" More giggles, and a boy ahead of us says, "Hey, that's enough! You want all of us to get in trouble!"

Someone is barking out some sort of command, and I crane my neck to see what it is all about. I see the big sixth-grader with the white armband, standing stiffly a few steps from the platform, facing the entire formation. Then, each class leader reports to the big boy that his class is all assembled and so on. The big boy turns around on his heels, salutes the teacher on the platform, and makes his report that the entire school is assembled and so forth. The teacher —the Teacher of the Day—returns the salute. The boy—the Student of the Day—pirouettes around, clicking the heels of his boots. Again facing the formation, he shouts, "At ease!"

It is all very much like a military formation, parade, and ceremony. The teacher on the platform is the battalion commander, the big boy is the battalion executive officer, the class leaders are the company commanders, and so on down the line. I am, then, a mere private or maybe a corporal. . . .

It strikes me then that I have not seen any Japanese children in the field. I discover later that they have their own morning assembly in another field in the back of the school.

It is obvious that we do not mix in classes. They have their
own classes and classrooms, and we have ours, although we
are all in the same school. A few years later, they will build
a new school somewhere outside the town, exclusively for
themselves.

The teacher on the platform is Japanese, and he is ad-
dressing the assembly. I do not understand what he is saying,
and I get the impression that the other second-graders and
first-graders do not understand him either. Many of them
are fidgeting, whispering to each other, and teasing one another. When the teacher has finished speaking, the Student
of the Day shouts out a command, and the entire formation
shuffles and rustles and faces what must be east, because we
are now all facing toward where the sun rises. Another command and everyone is bowing deeply—everyone except me.
The small boy next to me, bending from his waist, twists
his face toward me and whispers, "Bow your head or else
you are going to get a beating later on." There is urgency
in his hushed voice, and, after one quick look around me,
I lower my head, still not knowing what is going on. It is
the ritual of bowing toward where the Japanese Emperor
is supposed to be in his Imperial Palace in Tokyo—I find out
later. We are required to do this every morning. I tell my
father about it that evening, and he doesn't say a word,
though my mother says not to think about it too much and
just to do what other children do, because it would be a
shame to get beaten for something as silly as not bowing
one's head—for nothing, in short. I think about it, however.
Would the Japanese Emperor know that we children are
bowing our heads to him? He may be asleep . . . he may be
eating his breakfast . . . or he may be in the toilet, for all we
know . . . and I can't help giggling about the picture con-
jured up by the last image . . . the Emperor is in the toilet
and someone knocks on the door and says, "Your Majesty,
Your Majesty! The children, the children! They are bowing
to Your Majesty!" . . . and the Emperor says, "Wait a minute!

Wait a minute! I have my pants down!" Ha, ha, ha, I laugh;
I want to tell my parents about it but it is not a very nice
thing to say, so I decide to keep it to myself.

The morning assembly is over at last, and each class
marches into its classroom. It turns out that each class—and
there are two or three classes in each grade—has its own
room and teacher for a whole year; other teachers come in
to teach, depending on the subjects. Our classroom is a large
room at the end of a wooden building that has a long,
wooden corridor running the entire length of it. The room
has a nice view; on the left, it looks out on a small pond
with rocks and water lilies and another classroom building
identical to our building; to the right, beyond the corridor,
through the glass windows, we can see pine trees and, in between the branches, a little of the town below the hill. The
class leader seats me in one of the front seats squarely in
front of a small lectern on a platform. There is a large blackboard behind the lectern, and an enormous Japanese flag
hangs on the wall above the blackboard, which is framed,
on the right, by the school motto, in Chinese characters
written in black ink with brush, and, on the left, by the
national slogans, also in Chinese characters. Something about
"Long Live the Emperor" and "Long Live the Invincible
Imperial Forces," and so on. As I sit looking at these slogans,
the Invincible Imperial Forces are battering the Chinese,
having conquered most of the heartland of China. In Italy,
the Fascist Mussolini has been in power for years now, and,
in Germany, Hitler and his Nazis are firmly in control. Three
years ago, in 1935, Mussolini's Fascist armies conquered
Ethiopia, and, the next year, Ethiopia was "annexed" by Italy,
just as my country was "annexed" by Japan, by force, in 1910.
Japan's Imperial Army gobbled up Manchuria in 1934 and
invaded China proper in 1937. The same year, Japan, Germany, and Italy formed the so-called Axis powers—all set to
carve up the world. In 1938, the year I am starting at the new
school, Germany annexes Austria; and, in July of this same

year, the Japanese troops and the Soviet troops are fighting
along the Manchurian-Siberian border. In September, the
Munich Pact is signed by England, France, Germany, and
Italy, handing over Czechoslovakia's Sudetenland to Ger-
many; everyone in non-Axis countries is saying, "Peace in
Our Time," echoing Neville Chamberlain, who, as England's
Prime Minister, negotiates the Munich Pact to appease Hit-
ler. Peace in Our Time. . . . Only six months later, in 1939,
Germany will swallow up Czechoslovakia, Hungary, and Ru-
mania; Italy will try to "annex" Albania. In April, Hitler's
Germany will sign a nonaggression treaty with Poland, and,
in August, one with Soviet Russia—only to invade Poland in
September to ignite the Second World War. Meanwhile,
Peace in Our Time. . . .

And, meanwhile, here we are, the children of the second
grade, standing up in our classroom, reciting the Japanese
national slogans—Long Live the Sacred Emperor, Long Live
the Invincible Imperial Forces, Long Live the Conquest of
China by the Invincible Imperial Forces. . . . And there is a
huge map of China on the wall in the back of the classroom,
most of its heartland colored red and its cities pinned with
a little Japanese flag of the rising sun. On the left of the
back wall, there is another large map; this one is of Europe,
with Nazi Germany and its expanding territories colored
dark brown. Geography is changing, and we are hard put to
keep up with the changing of colors of countries, as the
armies of the Axis Powers, in the West and in the East,
continue to advance. The maps in our classroom are covered
with arrows, standing for these armies, that are thrusting out
and curling around like gigantic tentacles. Peace in Our
Time . . . and the children are singing martial songs of
the "Invincible Imperial Forces," songs celebrating the de-
feats and massacres of the enemy, and the brave deeds of the
Imperial soldiers who bayoneted to death over 4,000 Chinese
civilians in Nanking in December of 1937—the Rape of
Nanking.

So, that morning, the first day at the new school, I am sitting silently in one of the front seats, uneasy, uncomfortable, lonesome, and longing for the familiar sights and familiar friends and familiar warmth of familiar grown-ups. The children are unruly and loud. Books and notebooks are flying about and so are caps and rubber balls and anything else that can be thrown. The room has a sweaty odor from so many bare feet; to keep the room clean, we remove our shoes before entering the classroom, the floor of which is waxed shiny and slippery, and we leave our shoes outside the door on wooden shelves. I am wearing socks, and I notice that only very few children are wearing them. Most are barefoot, and the smell of their sneakers and rubber shoes, mixed with their sour body odor, is nauseating. A book bag lands on my small wooden desk, and another one hits me in the back of the head. I stand up, turn around, and glare at the children—bigger ones—in the back rows. Everything is quiet for a second before that big boy, who sits in a corner seat in the last row, squeezes his runny nose with his fingers and oink-oinks. The room is plunged into the same pandemonium as before. I am looking down, gazing into the rough surface of the desk top, my fingers tracing all the knife carvings, scratches, and pencil marks. Suddenly, everything is hushed. I look up from the desk and see a tall young man standing at the open door surveying the room. He is our teacher, a Korean.

We are all sitting silent and demure when the young teacher closes the door behind him and takes his seat on the platform behind the lectern. He looks around the room, and his eyes spot me finally and he nods with a smile.

Unlike the Japanese teachers, he wears his hair long and parted in the middle. His eyebrows are thick and dark. His large eyes and his high cheekbones lend to his pale face an air of poor health. I remember my grandfather telling me to be strong and healthy so I could walk down the street with my head high. . . . The teacher clasps his hands together on the lectern, and his hands are bony and his fingers are knobby. He clasps and unclasps his hands a few times, looking about him. The children are quiet. The teacher gets up and strides down the platform to the windows that look out toward the pond. He opens two windows. I don't feel any breeze coming in through the open windows—only the heavy, humid air. He returns to his seat, and begins to speak in a quiet, gentle voice that surprises me.

"As you all know," he says, "we have a new boy in our class this morning. His family has just returned from Manchuria. Some of you may know his father's name. Certainly, some of your parents would know who this boy's father is. I am good friends with his uncles in Tokyo, where we go to the same college. So, our new friend is no stranger to our town and certainly not to you, and I hope you will all be good friends and help each other. You do realize what it would be like if you were suddenly plucked out of this classroom and this school and transferred to a different school in a different province or country. You can certainly imagine how confusing and frustrating it would be on your first day in a new school. So, our new friend here must be a little confused and bewildered. We certainly do have rules and regulations that he must find strange and in many ways peculiar, and we must admit that we do have many peculiar ways we are supposed to do certain things. This, then, is the time when you all should try to be most helpful to our new friend. So, let's welcome our new friend to our class." With that, the teacher stands up and claps his hands and the children, jumping up from their chairs, clap their hands, too. I remain in my seat, head bowed, embarrassed, and rather happy. In a moment, all sit down. "And now," says the teacher, looking at me directly, "we, in this class, have a tradition, which is that a new student will sing a song for us as a way of concluding his introduction to the class. Would you, therefore, stand up, face the class, and sing us a song, your favorite song."

I am at a loss. I have not been told by my parents about this "tradition," and I am, therefore, not prepared for the ordeal. I stand and look up at the teacher, who says, "Turn around and look at your classmates now. Let's hear your favorite song."

I turn around. Faces and faces, all blurred to my eyes, waver and sway all around me. The big boy in the corner—he has his thumb and forefinger in front of his face, ready to squeeze his nose and say oink . . . I stare at the back wall and then the large map of Europe, and my gaze shifts to the brown, wooden ceiling and then back to the map, and I concentrate on the map as if I have been asked to recite the names of the many little countries in Europe, thinking I must sing, I must sing my favorite song . . . but I have so many favorite songs, and I think about all the songs I know and can sing and have sung . . . I have sung with my friends in Manchuria, my familiar friends in Manchuria, with whom, only a week before, I was playing and singing, all those friends I have left behind in Manchuria—Korean, Chinese, Canadian, American, English friends . . . and I remember all their faces and gestures and the songs we sang together. And, then, without realizing it, I am singing, first quietly, haltingly, then loudly, being carried away, by then knowing that I am singing, all the time thinking about my friends in Manchuria and looking at the map of Europe, finding England and Ireland there and thinking especially about that chestnut-haired boy—was he English or Irish? (I never knew the difference) —and I am singing, in English, "Danny Boy, Oh, Danny Boy . . ." I am halfway into the song and now, emboldened, I can look the children fully in their faces, one by one, and, to my horror, I see them covering their ears with their hands, staring up at the ceiling . . . and I quickly look toward the big boy in the corner, and I see him, quiet and unmoving, his face held in his hands, his elbows propped on the desk top, and he is listening to my singing, his attention rapt and unwavering. When

I finish singing, the big boy claps his hands first, even before the teacher behind me does. The children clap their
hands. I turn around and sit down and dare not look up at
the teacher.

"That was very nice," he says. "It certainly was unusual,
and I am sure we all enjoyed the song, although most of
us here do not understand English. Well, children, we will
have to learn the song. I know the Korean words for it, and
someday we may sing it together. Let me see if I can tell
you a little bit about the song. . . ."

I am not listening to him. I am thinking of the farewell
party at our school in Manchuria, with all the children and
their parents.

The party is given by the children of the missionaries. I
and my little sister are the guests of honor; the party is for
us—the next day we will be leaving the town to go back to
Korea. The grown-ups are having their own party in one
corner of the school hall, but they join the children when
the time comes for singing. Everyone sings. I sing "My Old
Kentucky Home"—my mother taught it to me and rehearsed
it with me the day before. A boy sings "I Dream of Jeannie
with the Light Brown Hair," and that English or Irish boy
and his sister sing "Danny Boy," and the song is for me. . . .
There is a big cake with small candles burning and twinkling,
and there is a large punch bowl filled with juice and slices
of fruit floating in it. When the farewell party is over, we all
hug each other, boys shaking hands and girls kissing each
other on the cheek. The grown-ups are hugging, shaking
hands, and kissing on the cheek, too. Many of them have
tears in their eyes, and a few women are quietly sobbing.
Although my family will be the first to leave the town, they
all know that, soon, everyone will have to leave and say
good-by. The missionary people have been harassed by the
Japanese and their Manchurian puppets, and, with the
Japanese invasion of the Chinese mainland in full operation,

the extraterritorial privileges given foreign missionaries by
the Chinese Government are no longer recognized, and
foreign governments cannot protect their citizens in this
part of the world. The situation in Europe is bad, and,
although Japan is not yet at war with America and England,
everyone knows that war will come sooner or later. The
missionaries have received word from their home countries
to prepare themselves for an eventual evacuation and, before
they must leave for home, they want to make sure their
Korean and Chinese friends will be looked after and spared
from Japanese threats and harassment. The farewell party
for my family is, then, a farewell party for all. "Oh, Danny
Boy" . . . and "I Dream of Jeannie with the Light Brown
Hair" . . .

And here I am, uprooted once again and transplanted
into what was once ours but is no longer—an alien land
that is not an alien land—finding myself cut off from my
friends, forlorn, bewildered, and melancholy. And I know
my eyes are filling with tears. I fight back the tears and
swallow a big lump in my throat.

The teacher is saying, ". . . so we shall have no class today.
You may go out to the field, and we shall assemble in twenty
minutes. Did you all bring the money I mentioned yesterday?"

The children say in unison, "Yes, sir."

He says to me, "Since you weren't here yesterday, I will
lend you the money, and you can bring it to me tomorrow."

The class is dismissed.

He comes over to me, taking out some coins from a small,
black leather wallet.

I tell him that I have some money with me but that I do
not understand why I need it.

He explains to me that the entire school will go to the
town theater to see a movie, actually an hour-long newsreel.
The children have been told to bring money to pay for the

admission. He looks around at the children who are quietly watching us and says that we will all get used to each other in no time, that he and one of my uncles went to the same high school and the same college in Tokyo, but he had to come home and teach for a while because his family needed him. "See you all out in the field," he says to everyone around and walks out of the classroom.

The children are running out of the room, whooping it up. Some of them stop behind me—I am still sitting in my seat—and tiptoe by, imitating my singing of "Danny Boy," twisting out some unintelligible words and wagging their tongues before dashing out of the room. A few others walk by me and quickly whisper "I liked your singing" or something to that effect. A boy—I can't tell what he looks like because I am not looking up from my desk—saunters by me, in a sort of measured step, and says, as if to himself, "It is not smart to sing foreign songs. . . ."

By now, almost everyone is out of the room, and, yet, the big boy hasn't gone out. I sit still, pretending I am rearranging the books, notebooks, and pencils in my book bag and making sure the buckles on the bag are secure. . . . The big boy is standing by my side. I glance at him and see that there is another boy behind him. The big boy says, "Are you going to the movie?"

I nod. "Are you?" The big boy sniffles a lot and, when he sniffles, his nose, which is rather pudgy, gets all wrinkly. He is stocky and has a big, chubby round face.

"Of course not. We've already seen it," he says triumphantly, and looks back at his friend, who grins.

"You've already seen it? How?"

"His father works in the theater," says the big boy, thumbing back at the other boy. "So he sneaked us in the day before. It's all about the Japanese soldiers marching and fighting and something like that."

"So, why waste money on a movie you've already seen?"

says the other boy. "Do you want to see it?" He is short, and has a well-scrubbed baby face.

"I don't know," I say, standing up. "I guess I will have to go."

"Yeah " says the big boy, "if you haven't seen it, maybe you ought to see it."

I nod. "You followed me and my mother this morning, didn't you?"

"I wasn't following you," he says. "I was just coming to the school, and you were going the same way, that's all."

The other boy says, "We live a couple of houses from each other. You live in that big house up the hill, right?"

"Yes."

The big boy says, "That sure is a big house. I bet you have lots of rooms."

"Yes. If you come with me to the house someday, I will show you around."

"What are you doing after the movie?" says the shorter boy.

"I don't know. Going home, I guess."

They exchange a glance, and the big boy says, "We are going to skip the movie and go to swim. Do you want to come along with us?"

"Where do you swim?"

"In the river. Where else?" says the other boy, as if in despair at my ignorance.

"Well, he's a new boy in town. He doesn't know," says the big boy in my defense.

"Do you want to come?" says the other boy eagerly.

"I would like to. But I will have to tell my mother about it."

"Oh, do you have to tell your mother everything!"

"Sure he does," says the big boy. "Maybe his mother doesn't know where the river is. Got to tell his mother. On the first day, anyway."

"If my mother says all right," I say, "I would like to go
with you."

"That's settled, then," says the big boy. "We will meet
you later, outside the theater. All right? We will wait for
you."

I nod. "What about the lunch?"

"We've got our money for the movie," says the big boy.
"We can get some candies or something on the way to the
river."

"All right."

"You'd better go out to the field and join the class," says
the big boy. "We will see you later."

"All right."

The big boy says, "That was a nice song."

"I didn't know a word of it," says the other, "but it sure
sounded nice."

The big boy squeezes his nose with his fingers and lets
out, "Oink-oink." "Sounds much better than this!" He
laughs.

"Come on, you pumpkin!" shouts the other boy, squealing.

"See you!" "Pumpkin" and the other boy run out of the
room.

I am alone in the room, happy, glowing in the warm
feeling of knowing that I now have two new friends and
that we will be going for a swim in the river. I am not a
good swimmer, but I know they are, because of the way they
talked about it and because they are bigger than I am. I
can get my feet wet anyway. It is hot and humid, and it will
be nice to wade into the cool water up to my chest, at least,
and maybe the boys will teach me how to swim. In Manchuria, the winter is long and bitter cold, and everyone
skates, and I am a good skater. My father taught me how
to skate, and I have skated ever since I can remember. I
have a nice pair of skates, with real leather shoes and shiny,
long steel blades—a birthday present from one of the mis-

sionary people. I think that if these boys, although they may be good swimmers, can't skate, I can maybe teach them, come winter. . . .

I am gathering up my cap and the book bag when a big, tall man in a teacher's uniform strides into the room, accompanied by two small boys. The teacher has short, cropped hair and a big mustache. I stand up. He comes right up to me and stands glowering at me, his legs apart, his hands on his hips. His small eyes peer into mine and, taking me by surprise, he grabs my shoulder and wheels me around. I am face to face with the two small boys. The teacher says something to the boys in Japanese. One of them points a finger at me. I recognize him as one of the classmates. I don't know the other boy. The teacher shakes his head and shouts at me in Japanese, which I do not understand. I simply shake my head, meaning that I do not understand him, that I can't understand Japanese.

He slaps me on the cheek, so hard that I stagger and crumple back into my seat.

He pounces at me, pulls me up by the back of my neck, and when I am on my feet again, he slaps me again on the other cheek.

I do not know what is happening—why the teacher, a Japanese, is so angry at me and why I have to be slapped twice in front of the other boys. Tears flood out of my eyes, though I am not crying. . . .

I dare to look up at the big teacher—at his flushed, distorted face—and I see his mouth sputtering out Japanese words, high-pitched and rapid, and his mustache is jerking up and down. Out of the corner of my eyes, I see a couple of children peering into the room through the windows, then running away down the corridor.

The man is still screaming at me.

Again, I shake my head, my tears running into my mouth.

He slaps my face again, barking out a word, and again and again.

In despair, I look at the other boys.

One of them says, to my surprise, in Korean, "You are lying!"

In Korean, I stammer out, "I am not lying," though I do not know what I am saying or why I have to tell anyone that I am not lying.

The boy, the bigger of the two, says something in Japanese to the man, who, in turn, says something to the other boy, who I am by now sure is a Japanese boy. The Japanese boy runs out of the room.

I say again, in Korean, "I am not lying!"

The Korean boy says, "You are, too! I was in this room, and I heard you sing that foreign song in a foreign language!"

"What?"

The boy talks to the man, who sneers at me and says something in Japanese.

The boy snickers. "The teacher says your father is a criminal and that's why you are behaving like a criminal, too. Telling a lie to a teacher, ha!"

With that, I spring to my feet and leap at the boy. I am fast. My face lowered, my head smashes into his face, and I punch him in the stomach—the best way to fight, according to one of my uncles who is an officer in the Manchurian Army. He taught me this tactic on the sly, making me promise not to tell my mother about it.

I am punched on the cheek and flung onto the edge of the platform, not by the boy but by the teacher. He picks me up with one hand by gripping the front of my jacket and, with the other hand, slaps me on both cheeks. Then, he lets me go, pushing me down, and goes over to the boy. Through my tears and dizzying anger, I can see the boy is bleeding from the nose and the lip. He crouches on the floor between the desks and chairs. My stomach punch—my one-two punch.

The teacher turns to me, pointing his finger at the boy

crumpled on the floor, bleeding, as if to say, "Look what you've done to him!"

I wipe my tears off my face, feeling that both my cheeks are burning, and I am screaming and screaming, trying hard to say, "What have you done to me!"

It is then that my teacher runs into the room, comes straight to me and helps me to my feet, looking into my face. Through the heavy mist of my tears which well up again on seeing him I can see that his eyes are angry and his high cheekbones are twitching. He swings around and shouts in Japanese at the Japanese teacher, who shouts back, waving his hand at the other boy, who is now up, not bothering to wipe the blood off himself. My teacher, in a fury, says something, his thumb jabbing at his own chest. He goes to the other boy and gives him his handkerchief and as he does so he bends down a little and, suddenly, the Japanese teacher kicks my teacher in the rear and my teacher bumps into the boy and then into chairs and desks and he lands flat on his face on the floor. The Japanese teacher turns around and starts for the door, when my teacher struggles up and says something to the Japanese. The Japanese wheels around a few steps away from the door, and the next thing I know my teacher is flying in the air, letting out an ear-splitting cry, his clenched fist outstretched, and he flings the Japanese against the wall by the door with a big thud; the Japanese staggers down to the floor but picks himself up quickly and charges against my teacher who, with a shrug of his shoulder, flings the Japanese up in the air and, at the same time, chops at his neck with his hand. The Japanese thumps down onto a desk with a beastly moan and rolls off the desk onto the floor; he does not move for a while; then his hands grope for support, and he pushes himself up. He turns around to look at us, muttering something incomprehensible, gasping for air. The boy is cowering in the corner next to the door and, as my teacher approaches him, he raises his arms, covering his face with his hands, saying, "Please don't hit me!

Please don't hit me!" My teacher gazes at him for a moment. "In the old days, someone like you would have had his tongue cut out," he says. "I am not going to punish you. As you grow up, you will have to live with your conscience."

He turns to me. "Get your things. I will take you home."

I pick up my bag and cap and follow him out of the room, leaving behind us the Japanese teacher and the Korean boy. I put my shoes on. The corridor is swarming with children, some from my class, and they all hush up as we walk down the corridor. They know what happened. We walk out of the building, into the steaming sunshine. My cheeks are aflame, and I can feel welts all over them, thick and long as earthworms. My lips are cut and bleeding, and I can't move my jaw which, as if dislocated, is aching. The teacher dips his hands into the pond water and then puts his wet hands against my cheeks. I begin to cry. "There, there," he says, as I struggle to choke off my crying and to calm my shoulders that are violently heaving. "Go on and cry," he says. "It's all right. Cry it out. There, there."

We go out through the main gate of the school and silently walk down the hill. Once in a while, I look up at him. He is holding his head high, as though staring at the hazy blue sky. I keep pace with him by his side, and, suddenly realizing that I am going home and will see my mother, I reach out and hold his hand. He stops and looks down at me for a moment, and he squeezes my hand, tears shining in his eyes, though he is smiling.

"Come on," he says. "I'll give you a treat."

I mumble something about the movie.

Without looking at me, he says sharply, "You are not missing anything. Besides, your father wouldn't have approved of your seeing that movie, if he had a choice."

I do not understand what he says, only that he respects my father. I am thinking more of my new friends, who will be waiting for me outside the theater to take me to the river for a swim. I think I won't tell the teacher about them, because they were going to skip the movie; though, from what the teacher has just said, maybe the boys are doing the right thing. . . .

We are down the hill and at the edge of the plaza, and the teacher takes me into the Chinese restaurant. It is a small, rather dingy place, dark inside, with a dozen or so wooden tables and chairs. It smells good and familiar, like those restaurants in Manchuria, with the smell of soy sauce and steaming dough, of meat cooking and food frying. We sit at a table, facing each other "man to man." An old Chinese with an apron around his waist comes to our table. The teacher orders in Chinese, and I know he asks for six steamed cakes with meat and vegetables inside. Though it is only mid-morning, I am hungry and I can taste the cakes already. He pours hot tea for me. The Chinese man brings the cakes and sauce to dip them in. He talks with my teacher, and I can understand a little: They are talking about me—something about my fight, about the Japanese teacher's hitting me, and about my having lived in Manchuria. The Chinese man pats my head and says in Korean, "Your father—a good man. You—a good, strong boy." He is beaming, urging me to eat.

When we are ready to go out of the restaurant, the old man wraps up four cakes in white paper and hands them to me. He is insistent, and I take the cakes; they feel warm and moist through the paper. I think of my new friends and decide that I will give them the cakes when I see them, though I am not sure I will see them during the day. I thank the old man, who says in Korean, "Come again. Any time."

* * *

I am in bed. I have a splitting headache, and my face is swelling up. I also have, inside my mouth, a big cut that I did not notice before, and I keep tasting salty blood. My mother puts ointment on my face, not saying a word, and my grandmother makes me a glass of ice water with honey in it. My grandmother is a tiny woman, efficient, bustling, and always cooking something for the children. Her hair is as shiny and black as my mother's, though her face and hands are wrinkled. She sits by my bed, watching me drink the ice water. She wants to make more of it for me. My sister is out with the maid. The teacher has gone; he will come back later to see how I am doing. Mother knows about everything. My grandmother is back in the kitchen, and I can hear her chipping ice. My mother goes out to the kitchen and comes back with ice chips wrapped in a towel and puts them on my forehead. Her eyes are red. "Try to sleep," she says. I close my eyes. Suddenly, I feel limp and drowsy. I am home. . . . I am falling into sleep. My mother holds my hand in hers, and I can feel her long fingers tracing mine and hear her muffled sobs. With eyes closed, I say, "I am all right. I feel fine. It doesn't really hurt." She is quiet, and I am almost asleep when, with a sniffle, she abruptly leaves me and goes out of the room.

My mother is waking me up. I do not know how long I have slept. She is saying, "Your friends are here to see you." I open my eyes. It is bright in the room, and I feel a little dizzy, staring at the white ceiling. My grandmother is beside me, holding a large fan. I touch my cheeks. "Don't," my mother says. The ointment is still there, and I feel my face all puffed up. She wipes my fingers with a towel. "Your friends came to see you. Do you want to see them?"

"I made two new friends at the school today."

"There are four boys in the courtyard and about ten more outside the gate," she says. "You made lots of friends today."

"I don't know that many boys." I sit up. My back is in pain, as if it has been crushed with a rock.

"Do you think you can get up?" says my grandmother. "Is it all right for him to get up?" she asks my mother. "I think he should see his friends," says my mother. I nod.

My grandmother says, "Nice of those boys to come to see you." She gets up. "Why don't you have them all come onto the porch," she says to my mother, and then to me: "I'll make them ice water with honey, too, and maybe a slice of watermelon." She goes out to the kitchen.

Soon, fourteen boys from my class, led by the big boy, "Pumpkin," are crowded into the porch. No one speaks. My grandmother comes in with a big pitcher of ice water with honey, and my mother carries in a tray of sliced watermelon—red ripe, with black seeds. The boys are all sitting on the wooden floor, cross-legged, looking awkward and shy. They are waiting for my grandmother and my mother to go away. My grandmother goes around, pouring more ice water for them, saying, "Drink it up, boys. I can make more. It's such a hot day, and you must be dying of thirst. It really is very thoughtful of you all to come to see our boy." She turns to my mother. "Isn't it an extraordinary thing for these boys to come to see him?" "Yes, Mother," says my mother, slicing another big watermelon. She says, "Well, we will leave you now, and thank you all for visiting us."

At last we are alone. Everyone is quiet for a while, looking at me. We are sitting in a big circle, and the big boy is sitting next to me, on my right, and his friend with the baby face is on my left. We eat all the watermelon slices, busily picking out the black seeds, drink up all the ice water, and soon there is nothing left to eat or drink.

"Would you like more ice water?" I say. "And more watermelon?"

Everyone shakes his head. Silence.

Someone says finally, "Hey, Pumpkin, say something."

Pumpkin says, "Well, the three of us"—thumbing at me

and at his friend on my left—"were going to go to the river for a swim. He was going to meet us at the theater after the movie, so we went to the theater to wait for him while you were all watching the movie. We didn't know he wasn't there, and, then, you all come out of the theater, and he isn't there. Then, someone told us he had a fight and got beaten up by a Japanese teacher, and everything. So, we went back to the school, but he wasn't there either. Then, I saw our teacher in the marketplace, and he told me what happened. I mean, the teacher told us he was home and wouldn't be able to go to the river. I told the teacher about the swim. Then—hey, how did we all get together anyway?"

Someone says, "Some of us heard about the fight when we came out of the movie and saw you two out there and saw you two going off. I guess we followed you. You know everything, Pumpkin. You find out everything in no time, so we followed you two."

"I heard you punched that boy really good," says a small boy in the corner. "I bet his father will beat him up for getting beaten up by you."

Everyone laughs.

"What does his father do?" I ask.

"He is a teacher at our school, didn't you know?"

"No."

Pumpkin says, "Did you all hear that our teacher flipped that Japanese teacher with just one finger?" He snaps his fingers. "Just like that!"

"He wears a black belt, you know," someone says. "I saw him practice Yoodo one day. Boy—was he great!"

Pumpkin says to me, "Where did you learn to box!"

I tell them about my uncle in the Manchurian Army. He will be home in a few days on leave; they can all come and meet him; maybe he will let them touch his saber and pistol.

"Wow!" says a boy. "Have you ever fired his pistol?"

"Sure."

"You ought to be the class leader," says Pumpkin, looking serious. "Our teacher told us you got the highest score on the transfer test, and you beat that boy up, too. Yeah, you ought to be the class leader."

"I bet the Japanese teachers won't make him the class leader, though."

Pumpkin goes, "Oink-oink."

Everyone is laughing and oink-oinking.

My mother comes in. "Well, what's so funny?"

Everyone is looking demure and serious.

I tell her about the swim in the river.

Before she can say anything, everyone starts saying this and that about a swim in the river—that we will all go to the river together and that we will all be very, very careful.

"Well, that's very nice," she says, "but I think he should stay home today. The doctor is coming to take a look at him in a little while, and his face is still quite swollen. Another day, all right? But why don't you go and have a swim? I am sure he wouldn't mind if you all went without him today, so long as he knows he can go with you all another day. All right?"

"Yes, Ma'am," several say in unison, getting up.

"Take care of yourself," says Pumpkin, giving me a brotherly tap on the back. "Do you think you can come to school tomorrow?"

"Sure."

"Well, we will see you," says my mother.

They all bow to her as they leave the porch, one by one. I remember the steamed Chinese cakes, but there are only four of them, and I don't know what to do. Outside, in the courtyard, they wave and shout good-by. My grandmother comes out of the kitchen and says, "Come again, all of you." They bow to her and troop out the gate.

I call out, "Hey—Pumpkin! Wait a second!"

He comes back into the courtyard, trailed by his friend.

I do not want the other boys to hear me, so I whisper to Pumpkin when he comes close to me. I tell him about the Chinese cakes.

My mother, overhearing our conversation, says, "Well, why don't you ask him to come back later with his friend? I'll have them warmed up."

"All right, we'll come back after the swim in the river. See you later," he says and runs out, racing with his friend.

"Now, you'd better get back into bed," she says.

"I feel all right. It isn't hurting now."

"I know, I know," she says, firmly taking hold of my arm. "Come on. Back to bed."

I wake up again. It is dark. My father is beside my bed. I sit up.

"How do you feel?" he asks.

"I am all right, sir."

"You don't have to tell me anything. I know."

"That boy called you a criminal. . . ."

"Do you think your father is a criminal?"

"Of course not, sir."

"Well, that's what matters. But the Japanese think I am," he says, looking into my eyes. "I was in their prison when I was young. Before you came along. Before your mother and I were married."

"Was that when you were in college, sir?"

He nods. "I was in prison many years."

"Why, sir?"

"I can't tell you about that now. It is not time yet for you to know everything and to understand it all. Time will come. Someday, I promise, I will tell you about it. Now, all you have to know at this time is that I have done nothing in my life that you should be ashamed of. Do you understand that?"

"Yes, sir."

"That's all you need to know. Will you believe me? That, as my son, you have nothing to be ashamed of?"

"Yes, sir."

"All right. Do you think you would like to have dinner?"

"Yes, sir."

"Good. Your grandfather would like to have dinner with you and me. He's been waiting for you to wake up."

I get up and follow him to my grandfather's room.

I kneel down on the floor and bow to my grandfather.

He does not say anything.

My mother and the young maid bring in our dinner and set the table. It is unusual; my grandfather usually eats alone. The dinner is unusual, too; there is chicken—we have chicken only when we have guests or when it is someone's birthday—and there is a big dish of fried meat dumplings, my grandmother's specialty and my father's favorite, as well as mine.

My grandfather looks grave, and he is staring at my swollen face. When the table has been set and my mother and the maid have gone out of the room, we sit at the round table. Just the men in the family. My grandfather calls out to the kitchen, "Where is the wine?"

My mother comes in with a bottle of warmed rice wine and two small cups. She sets them on the table by my father.

My grandfather waits till she is out of the room; then, he stands up, goes over to a cupboard built into the wall, and returns with another small cup, which he places on the table in front of me. "I know your mother won't approve of this. . . ." He reaches for the wine bottle and pours the wine into the three cups on the table.

I glance at my father, who is silent and sitting still.

My grandfather raises his cup.

My father raises his cup, saying to me, "You, too."

I raise my cup. The sweet and sour smell of the warm wine makes my nose tingle.

"Drink it up now," says my grandfather.

We drink. I swallow it down with no difficulty, feeling warm in the throat and chest as the wine goes down, feeling big and strong, and feeling quite unabashedly happy.

My father looks at me for a moment and smiles.

"It tastes good," I announce to both of them.

My father laughs and rumples my hair with his big hand. "Now, it is your turn to pour the wine for your grandfather," he says.

My grandfather holds his cup in one hand, and I pour the wine into it, holding the bottle in both hands.

He drains his cup down, then picks up the bottle in one hand and fills my father's cup, which he is holding in both hands. That is the way the grown-ups drink wine. My cup stands empty, and my father tells me to turn it upside down on the table—that means you have had enough.

"Eat, boy, eat!" says my grandfather. "You must be strong and healthy. It seems as though you've got something besides brains, and that's good, too. Eat, boy, eat!"

The men of the family are having their dinner. . . .

In the middle of our dinner, we have a guest—my teacher. Though he insists that he will wait outside until we are finished with the dinner, my grandfather commands him to join us at the table. My father, who is out of the room with the teacher, brings him in.

I stand up and bow to him and, looking up, see that his face is as swollen as mine. One of his eyes is blue and purple and half-closed. His lips are cut and puffed up. He has a white bandage on his forehead.

He kneels down on the floor and bows deeply to my grandfather.

My father says, "He was taken to the police station this afternoon, and he just got released."

My grandfather stands up, goes over to the cupboard, and

brings another cup. Without a word, he fills the four cups on the table. "Come," he says to the teacher, who joins us at the table.

We drink the wine in silence.

My grandfather gives his own cup to the teacher and fills it for him.

My teacher drinks it down, returns the cup to my grandfather, and fills it for him.

My father then gives his cup to the young teacher, who drinks the wine in it, returns it to my father, and fills it for him.

"Have some dinner," says my grandfather, after a few rounds of wine.

"No, thank you, sir," the young man says. "I am not hungry."

"Have some," says my father.

My mother comes in with a bowl of chicken soup with meat dumplings in it. She puts it down before the young man. Her eyes are wet, and she avoids looking at my teacher.

When she is out of the room, my father says, "I am sorry."

My teacher bows to him.

"How is your mother these days?" asks my grandfather.

"She is improving. The doctor says she will be able to get up in a week or so."

"That's good," says my grandfather. "Is there anything we can do?"

"No, thank you, sir. We are fine."

Silence for a while. The chicken soup goes untouched.

My teacher says abruptly, "I came to say good-by, sir."

Silence again.

My father says, "What is your plan?"

"That's what I came to see you about, sir."

"Anything I can do, just tell me."

"I am thinking of going to Manchuria, sir, so I thought, perhaps, I could go to see your brother there. What do you advise me, sir?"

I understand he is speaking of my uncle in the Manchurian Army.

"What will you do then?" asks my grandfather.

"Well, sir . . ." My teacher looks at me quickly.

My father says, "As a matter of fact, the boy's uncle will be home in a few days, on leave. He will stay here for a week or so before he goes to his new assignment, near the Mongolian border. Do you think you understand what I am talking about?"

"Yes, sir. I do."

"What do you think of this?" says my father. "Can you wait a few more days, until the boy's uncle gets here? I am thinking, perhaps you can go with him to Manchuria. His being an officer will be helpful, if you know what I mean."

"I understand that, sir. I didn't know he was coming home. Yes, sir. If you think he wouldn't mind . . ."

"Of course, he wouldn't mind," says my grandfather.

"What about your mother?" asks my father. "Will your brother be able to look after her?"

"Yes, sir. I've already talked it over with him and with my mother, too."

"You needn't worry about your mother. She will be all right," says my grandfather, nodding his head. "Eat your soup now, before it gets cold."

"Thank you, sir." He picks up a spoon.

My father looks at me and says gently but very firmly, "You may be excused now. I want you to go to bed early."

I get up, bow to everyone, mumble my thanks and regrets to my teacher, and withdraw from the room.

"Please close the window on your way out," says my father.

I do, and, somehow, I know that they are going to discuss something very important, something so important that only the grown-ups should hear and talk about it. I do not mind being excluded; after all, I have had a drink of wine with all of them in there—just the men.

I go to my mother in her room. My sister is sleeping in the corner bed. My mother sits by a lamp, reading a newspaper.

"How many cups did *you* have?" my mother asks, giving me a sidelong glance.

"Two."

"Well!" she says, half-serious and half-mocking. "Wait till your other grandfather hears about that!"

"I feel fine."

"I am sure you do. How's your face? It is still swollen. Do you feel pain?"

"I am all right."

"I am sorry about what happened to your teacher."

"Will he be back at the school?"

"I imagine not. Not after everything that happened today."

"They are talking about my uncle in Manchuria."

"Yes, I know."

"He is going to go to Manchuria with my uncle."

"I know. Maybe you'd better not tell other people about it too much."

"Why?"

"I wouldn't be able to tell you why. Besides, you don't have to know that. You'd better go to bed. School tomorrow, you know. You *are* going back to school, aren't you?"

"Of course, I am."

"The Japanese teachers may punish you and be mean to you."

"I don't mind."

"Are you sure?"

"I am sure. I have nothing to be ashamed of. Besides, I have lots of new friends now."

"You can go to a private school in Pyongyang if you like, you know. You can stay with your other grandparents and go to school there."

"No. I will then have to be away from you and father
and everyone."

"We can come and see you often, and you can come
home on weekends."

"I don't think so. I think I am going to like the school
here. I want to be the class leader, too."

"Of course, you do. Are you sure you wouldn't rather go
to another school, in Pyongyang? A private school? Without
Japanese teachers?"

"I am sure."

"All right. As long as you are sure."

"Yes, Mother." And I think of my friends. Everyone who
came to see me in the afternoon and the swim and Pumpkin
and, then, the steamed Chinese cakes with meat and vegetables inside them. . . . "I almost forgot, Mother. Have
Pumpkin and the other boy been here? They said they would
be back after the swim for the cakes. Remember?"

She does not answer.

"Do you still have the cakes?"

"No."

"Then—did they come?"

"The other boy did," she says, standing up. "I gave them
to him." She is going out of the room. "Come with me."

I follow her out of the room to the veranda. In my grandfather's room in the other wing of the L-shaped house, the
windows are closed, but I can see the three of them still at
the table talking. My mother stands in the shadow outside
the room, by the window. "Come here," she says.

I go up to her.

"Something happened to your friend."

"You mean—Pumpkin?" It strikes me that I do not know
his name.

She nods. "The other boy came here. He was crying. He
told me that, when they got to the river—it was very hot.
Remember? When they got to the river, your friend Pumpkin
—well, he just ran ahead of everyone, put his bathing suit

on, and dove into the water. From a rock. Just like that. And that's the last they saw of him."

"What happened?"

"He dove into the water from the rock. They saw him dive, but, when they got there, they couldn't find him."

"You mean—he was still in the water? Like swimming underwater?"

"No. He just never came out of the water. Not for a long time."

"Where was he?"

"They looked for him there, but he couldn't be found."

"Was he drowned, then?"

"Yes. They found his body later, downstream."

"He is dead, then."

"Yes. I am sorry. It is a terrible thing."

"He is dead, then."

Without a word, she puts her arms around me.

I do not really understand my own words. I do know about drowning. . . . "He is not alive, then."

"He is dead," she says.

"Dead."

*   *   *

. . . And my young teacher is dead, too. My uncle helps him to cross the Manchurian-Mongolian border. He makes his way inside Mongolia. He is captured by the Soviet troops. The Russians kill him. Before they shoot him, they tell him that he is a Japanese spy.

Once upon a Time, on a Sunday

"Wake up," my mother whispers. "Wake up. This is Sunday, you know, and you have a lot of things to do today."

I am awake—I have been awake for some time, basking in the glorious sunshine that seeps through the pale blue curtains on the window in my room, letting it touch my bare feet and make them feel warm and toasty, and, once in a while, peeking out the window to see if I can catch a glimpse of my father. I know this is Sunday, and that is why I am still lazing around in bed, pretending to be asleep when my mother comes into my room to wake me up.

"Wake up now," she says a little louder, aware that I am only feigning not to hear her. "Your father is up and working already, and here you are being lazy. Tut, tut. Come on."

I toss in the bed, grunting, to make sure that it looks as if I am really just waking up, against my will, however. I take my time, though, keeping my eyes shut tight, toss around and roll over once or twice, then open my eyes, rubbing them hard with my hands to show her that they feel as though glued together . . .

But she is already gone from my room. She is, I admit to myself rather reluctantly, getting used to the theatrics I put on every Sunday morning for her benefit. I get up and open the curtains and the window. It is quiet outside, and the azure sky is cloudless. A cool breeze, rustling the leaves of the trees outside, leaps into the room, waving aside the open curtains. I don't see my father outside. I can't hear him either, but I can hear my mother in the kitchen slicing something on a cutting board—click, click, click. "My little sister must be still sleeping," I think, because, if she is up, I wouldn't fail to hear her jabbering around all over the place, trying to engage my mother—or my father, if he is unfortunate enough to be around—in an endless, nonsensical conversation. My mother is going to have a baby in a few months, and I am certain it is going to be a boy, and— ha!—that'll teach the little girl. . . . Just then, I hear my little sister in the kitchen—jabbering away.

It is summer, toward the end of August, sadly enough, but the school is still on vacation for another week or so. In the summer, my parents and we, the children, go out to our apple orchard and live in the cottage my father built on a small knoll in the middle of the orchard. My grandparents stay in the main house in town, coming out to see us once in a while—only once in a while because we go into town every Sunday morning and, also, on market days. I don't mind getting up early on market days when we all go into town, where I am allowed to roam about in the crowded, bustling open-air market, with two coins, my allowance, to do whatever I please with. Going into town is half of the fun and excitement on market days.

My mother and sister ride on an oxcart, "chauffeured" by one of the younger tenant farmers, while my father and I ride our bicycles. I got my own bicycle when I moved up to the third grade and became the leader of my class; it was a present from my maternal uncles, all three of them—one a concert singer, another an actor, and the youngest a concert

pianist. "A very artistic, otherworldly family your mother
has," says my father often, teasing her. "All up on the stage!
What would you all have done if man hadn't invented art!"
He doesn't quite dare to bring my maternal grandfather, a
theologian and minister, into it. She would reply, teasing
back, "We would be down to earth like your family is,"
meaning, of course, my father's family—or my grandfather
and father, anyway—which is a farming family. My paternal
uncles, the three of them, are more down to earth, really,
than my maternal uncles—one of them is a student of political
science, now working for a farmers' cooperative; another is a
soldier; and the third is an executive of a trading company
in China. Anyway, my mother, the eldest daughter in a very
artistic family, is riding on an oxcart with my sister, both of
them holding parasols to shade themselves from the hot sun,
mother's pink parasol giving a soft, shimmering pink tint to
her face and her white blouse and pale blue skirt, and my
little sister's multicolored toy parasol, as she twirls it around
and around, engulfing her in a weird conglomeration of red,
orange, green, and blue. The farmer rides in the front, a big
straw hat nearly covering his bronze-red face. He holds the
reins in his hands, though he rarely has to use them, because
the big, fat, sturdy animal, his deep tan hide glistening and
his mouth foaming and drooling white saliva, knows the way
by heart as he plods along, unhurried, nonchalant, and
staring ahead fixedly with his enormous bloodshot eyes, only
occasionally swinging his tail to chase the buzzing flies away.
And, if the flies are too persistent, the farmer reaches over in
his seat for a swatter and goes slap, slap! on the big rump of
the animal. . . .

And the oxcart goes creak, creak over the bumpy, rutted
dirt road leading out of our apple orchard, past farmers'
houses that always have something—pale green gourds,
red peppers, white radishes—drying on their straw-thatched
roofs, and past the farmers and their wives and children, and
I can see the parasols tilting and swaying as the oxcart rolls

along. As soon as we are on the new main road, which at least is smooth, though not paved, I can almost hear my mother give out a deep sigh of relief as she straightens up in her seat. My father then waves at her and little sister, telling me to stay with them, and shoots forward on his bicycle and goes fast down the road, as if he has been waiting for days for the opportunity to show how fast he can ride on his bicycle. Actually, he has to be at the market early to supervise the selling and buying and so on. I ride alongside the oxcart, demonstrating, on my part, my dexterity, going zigzag and looping around and going fast and stopping quickly, ignoring my sister, who, I know, is making derogatory comments to my mother about me. I go forward fast when I see a sharp curve ahead, until they lose sight of me; then, I hide in the bush or behind a clump of trees and wait for them to pass by, and I take my time so they will begin to wonder where I am, and then I appear behind them, as if out of nowhere, casual and whistling—that is, until I run out of breath and strength. I then ask the driver to stop the cart, and he comes down and puts my bicycle onto the back of the cart and helps me hop in. I sit apart from my mother and my sister, ignoring them, as if to say that I could really have gone with my father but for his instructions to stay with them, and, well, here I am. . . . My mother hands me an apple or a piece of candy sometimes, and I tilt my straw hat back and try to look grown up and, therefore, wise and go forward to sit next to the farmer on the driver's seat. I snap in two the long stick of candy, which has become sticky in my hands, and give a piece to the driver, who grins and pops it into his mouth, crunching the whole thing, and we plod on. . . .

But it is not a market day. It is Sunday—and I have grown to dislike Sundays. Usually, on any other day during the vacation, my mother would let me sleep as long as I want, but a Sunday is a Sunday, and we have to get up early to make sure that my parents and my sister get to our church,

the only Presbyterian church in our town, in time for my
mother, who is the church pianist, to practice a little with
the choir; also, we get up early to make doubly sure that
I get to my school. All the school children who are neither
sick—with a doctor's permission—nor out of town—with a
teacher's permission—must attend the Sunday-morning assembly, a regular phenomenon at the school all year around,
for a long lecture by the Japanese principal, usually on the
progress of the Imperial Army occupying this and capturing
that in China and on how we must all do this and that to
match ourselves with the Imperial soldiers at the front, and
so forth. Then, we have an hour of calisthenics, designed to
help us grow up strong and healthy, both in mind and
body, in order to be able to offer ourselves someday to the
sacred tasks demanded by the Emperor of all the loyal subjects of the colony. After that, we hand in our weekly homework assignment to our teacher, and, then, the other children
are allowed to go home, but the class leaders stay. The class
leaders must remain and perform whatever duties the
teachers assign them, such as grading the children's homework or visiting on behalf of the teachers the children who
are supposed to be sick, mainly to collect certificates of their
illnesses or, as is often my case, to run various errands for
the teacher, "just to keep you away from the church," according to my grandmother. For that matter, all Christian children in our town—Presbyterian, Catholic, Methodist, Baptist,
Seventh Day Adventist—are unable to attend their churches
because of the Sunday-morning assembly at the school. "Like
leeches," says my grandmother, "the Japanese won't leave
the children alone, even on Sundays."

I do miss out on a lot of games with other children on
Sundays, after the morning assembly. Many a time, I want to
decline the unwanted honor and ill-fated privilege of being
the leader of my class, but my teacher won't hear of it. He is
a thirty-two-year-old Korean who is quite pro-Japanese,
though he comes to our house once in a while to pay his

respects to my father—to "play it safe and look good on all sides, just in case," according to my grandfather, who never offers his wine cup to him. "It is the principal himself who appoints all the class leaders, you know," says the teacher blandly, grinning rather condescendingly. "Anyway, you are the best student in the class, you get the highest grades, and everybody in the class wants you to be the class leader. Besides, it is a great honor, you know." I can hardly think it an honor to spend my Sundays running errands for him and, often, for other teachers and going around collecting sick reports from bed-ridden children. I even think of not studying too much, so that my grades will go down, but, when I suggest that way out of my predicament, no one in the family has the heart to tell me, "That's right. Don't study too hard, and don't try to pass the tests." My father says, rather enigmatically, though a little sadly, "There are other reasons for your being the class leader. You'll see. But, you shouldn't let it depress you that much, should you?" I don't see the "other reasons" for the dubious distinction of being the leader of my class, but, I will soon have a chance to find them out for myself. . . .

So—this is Sunday. I dress quickly and dash out of the cottage before my little sister has a chance to pester me with silly questions about such things as what I am doing and what I am going to do. The cottage, as I said, is on a small knoll right in the middle of the orchard, and, from the cottage, I can see the whole range of the orchard, which spreads out on a more or less circular flatland, which is fringed on all sides by rising mountains. I stand by the small flower bed in front of the cottage and look around. To my right, where a dirt road leads out from the orchard past several cottages that my father has built for our tenant farmers, there is a gate, a main entrance to the orchard. On one of the gate posts, there is a white wooden board bearing the name of the orchard—New Life Apple Orchard—which, according to my mother, "has several meanings." Just inside the gate, there is a row of chicken coops and a huge pigsty and a separate building for cows and oxen. A narrow dirt path veers off the main path into the orchard and crawls up the knoll to our cottage. To the left, down the knoll, is a small stream, where we take a dip and splash around in the ever gurgling cool water under the green canopy of the leaves of the trees; often at night, I lie awake, listening to the rippling water's whispering that comes through the tumultuous chirping and croaking of crickets and frogs and all those little things that come out at night. By the flower bed, there is a little stone terrace, which is covered with an overhang of vines that makes a natural sunshade.

We sometimes have our lunch on the terrace, under the vines, or sit out there in the evening, drinking tea, watching the sunset, until the sweet and pungent smoke of the green incense (which keeps mosquitos and gnats off) wafts away into the gathering darkness and blends with the bluish gray mist that drifts in and hangs over the apple trees, and my father puts out the red, glowing ember of the incense, and my mother goes inside and lights kerosene lanterns. Yellowish light shines out of the windows, rendering the darkness outside darker and a little forbidding, and we can see my mother inside, letting down mosquito nets over our beds. . . .

I am now standing on the stone terrace, looking for my father, who is somewhere in the middle of the orchard, but I can't find him. The apple trees' leaves are soft green and radiant in the bright morning sun, their branches drooping, heavy with all those apples. In the spring, when the trees blossom white and pinkish, I can't see their branches or trunks from the cottage; the panorama is spectacular, and all I can see is an undulating ceiling of white and green and pink as far as my eyes can reach. With the towering rocky mountains giving it an air of security and remoteness from the outside world, the beautiful orchard basks in its own quietness and dignity and, of course, its fertility. My father and I often stroll in the orchard, walking by rows and rows of apple trees, looking at thousands and millions of tiny green buds, and my father says, "It takes years and years for apple trees to grow big and strong enough to create apples, and years and years of hard work to help them grow." Bees humming and buzzing, wild rabbits dashing in and out of bushes, and all that is nature astir in the early morning— and I take my father's rough, weathered hand, remembering the time he wept openly when the orchard was ruined by a sudden, violent out-of-season hailstorm, and I trot along, happy and proud. . . .

I take a chair from under the vines and stand on it to see if I can find my father. My sister comes out of the kitchen with a pair of binoculars. "What are you doing with Father's binoculars?" I say to her. "You don't even know how to adjust the lenses."

"I know how," she says. "I am going to find Father with these." She comes beside me and looks through the binoculars, scanning the orchard down below.

"What do you think you are doing?" I say. "Spying on him or something, like that Japanese detective snooping around our house?"

"You are just being mean!"

"Give them to me."

"I will not!"

"Oh, come on. Please?"

My mother calls out from the kitchen. "You'd better call your father. We must be going."

I shout out, as loud as I can, "Father! Father!"

My sister squeaks, "Father! Mother says we must be going!"

Our voices spread out through the orchard and quickly come back to us in waves of echoes. There is a moment of silence before my father's voice is heard in the orchard: "I am coming!"

We shout back.

He replies.

Echoes of all our voices ring out again and again.

"That's enough, now," says my mother, emerging from the kitchen. "You'd better come inside and wash up."

My sister hands me the binoculars and runs inside. I stay outside and look through the binoculars for my father. I spot him between the rows of trees to the left of the cottage. Seen through the binoculars from where I am, it is as if he is in a slow-motion silent movie. His dark brown arms are raised above him, as he examines a branch; his white shirt looks whiter against the reddish brown of the back of his neck; he starts walking, slowly, looking at the trees this way and that; he carries a long stick with which he taps the tree trunks or lifts up a branch; the bottoms of his white trousers must be wet from the dew on the grass. He can see me now, and he waves his arm and swings his stick in the air. He is coming up the path. . . .

*   *   *

On a day like this, that is, on Sundays when, unless it rains, we go into town, we have breakfast with my grandparents. As usual, my grandmother is up early and bustling around in the kitchen, preparing our breakfast—frying this, boiling that, tasting the soup that we have with every meal, making sure the rice is cooked just right to suit my grandfather, who likes it on the moist side. Unlike my mother, my grandmother never thinks she has cooked enough to feed everyone, and she enjoys serving big meals; for example, this morning's breakfast: spinach soup with beef in it, fried eggs for my father and me, boiled eggs for everyone else, fried squash, fried beef slices, fried fish, boiled and salted fish eggs, pickled cucumber, spiced eggplant, pickled Chinese cabbage, spiced bean sprouts, fried bean curd, dried sea weed—oiled, salted, and sautéed—and, of course, rice; then, there is an assortment of summer fruit. My grandmother can never sit still during meals, because she simply has to make sure that everyone is having plenty and that every dish is replenished as soon as the food in it has been consumed. Feeding the family is her life's mission, and this she goes about accomplishing with determination and stamina and, naturally, great joy.

But this morning, we are a little late in getting started from the orchard, and so I rush through my breakfast, under the watchful eyes of my grandmother, who does not approve of hasty eating, and I dash out of the house, not giving her time to wrap something up—a piece of cake, sticks of candy, or fruit—for me to take with me, "either for yourself or for your friends."

At this moment, I am actually anxious to get to the school as quickly as I can. There is one thing good about the Sunday-morning assembly, because I can see my friends and exchange information about what everyone has done during the week and what everyone is planning to do in the coming week, and so on. The only chance I have to talk and play with them a little comes before the assembly, so I want to get there early, before the teachers start trooping out of the principal's office, where they have their own assembly. During the vacation, there is one exception to the rules for the Sunday-morning assembly: We don't have to wear our school uniform. It always amazes me, on Sunday mornings at the assembly, to look at everyone and suddenly realize that everyone wears different clothes, according to the different tastes of either the children themselves or, most likely, of their parents. Anyway, it is more colorful than a field full of black caps, black jackets, and so forth. Girls, naturally, look more colorful than boys, and each one looks suddenly unique and more distinct than she would as one of an identically clothed multitude.

Several of my friends in the fourth grade are telling me about their plan to fly kites in the afternoon. Kite-flying is really at its peak in the winter, around December and, especially, during the New Year holidays, but we have to do something besides homework, and we can't always go swim-

ming in the river. So, they are going to climb up the hill
beyond the school and fly kites. We all know how to make
our own kites. Making a kite is an art, and, among us, it is
considered absolutely out of one's class either to buy a kite
or to have a grown-up make one for him. I am regarded by
my friends as one of the kite experts in our class; that is, I
not only make my own beautiful kites of all designs but know
when to let out the string and when to reel it in, how much
to let out and when to give a pull or a tug to the string to
make the kite dip, dive, turn, and do all sorts of other
maneuvers. One must learn when to pull at the string in
order to take advantage of a string that is "reinforced" with
gluey paste mixed with pulverized glass, so that one is able
to cross the string with those of other kites and cut them off—
and that is the whole point in flying a "fighting kite," one
of those fast, agile, little, but tough, sharp-witted, mean
kites. . . .

I am standing in front of the bustling, chattering group of
my friends and the other children of my class. We all have
short hair, cropped so short that it looks as though it has
been shaved off our skulls, all of us looking like a bunch of
little Buddhist monks. The thought makes me laugh. A boy
ambles over to me.

"What's so funny?" he says, looking around. He is one of
the bigger boys in our class, a year or two older than most of
us. He joined the class in the third grade, coming to us from
a small school in one of the outlying villages. Tall and
husky, with a bullethead, he is not very bright and refined—
as some of my precocious friends would say—and, being un-
familiar with the life in town and unsure of himself among
the town children, he has somehow attached himself to me,
his class leader, and he makes a point of coming to me with
all sorts of questions and also of being seen with me when we
are in the presence of other children. I like him, however,
because I know what it is like to be a transfer student and

also because he is very strong, though a bit clumsy, and he often stays after school to help me clean and tidy up the classroom, which is, also, one of a class leader's many duties.

I tell him what I was laughing about.

"Hey, you're right," he says. He has a habit of always agreeing with me. He rubs his head with his hands and says, "Once, I saw a little boy-monk with a couple of big ones begging for food in our village. I think he was younger than I was, maybe six or seven, at most. Come to think of it, though, my big brother said that, once, he thought of running away and becoming a monk. That was before they took him away to the army, though."

"Took him away to the army . . ." The Japanese are now allowing Koreans to volunteer for their army. Special Volunteer Soldiers, they call those young Koreans. The boy's brother gets drunk one day and gets into an argument with a Korean detective working for the Japanese police and winds up beating up him and a Japanese policeman. The next thing he knows, he receives a notice from the local police that his application for volunteering for the army has been approved and that his village is honored to have produced a Special Volunteer Soldier, who is now allowed the privilege of fighting in the war alongside the Japanese soldiers, and so forth. He tries to run away from his village and is hunted down and caught and shipped off to China.

Four other classmates of mine have brothers and uncles who were sent to China as Special Volunteer Soldiers.

"Have you heard from your brother yet?" I ask.

He shakes his head. "No, nothing from him. Well, he doesn't know how to write anyway. He never went to school, you know. I am the only one in the family who's ever gone to school. My father says to my mother that, probably, the only time we'll ever hear about my brother is when he is dead."

I don't say anything for a while.

He seems to think about what he has told me. "If my
brother gets killed," he says, "I'll be the eldest son in the
family then. I guess."

"Come on," I say. "He will come back someday."

"I don't know," he says. He points a finger at one of the
boys in the class next to ours. "That boy's brother was already
killed in China. Did you know that?"

"No. When?"

"Who knows? Just a little urn with his ashes came back.
No telling whose ashes they really were, come to think of it."

I am uneasy and uncomfortable, suddenly thinking of my
uncle in the Manchurian Army. "Come on," I say to him.
"You'd better get back in your line."

Without a word, he takes out of his pocket a sling shot.
He gives it to me. "I made it myself. You want it? You can
have it."

I admire it. I am learning how to make one, but I have
not yet been too successful. "Don't you want it?"

"I made that for you," he says; then, in whispers: "Don't
tell the other boys." He trots away from me even before I can
thank him. His sneakers are dirty and tattered. His trousers
have big patches on the knees and on the seat.

Later on, I tell my father about the sling shot and about
the boy and his brother who is in China. A week later, when
I see the boy again, he tells me that my father's foreman has
been to his house with a box of apples and a big sack of rice.

"White rice," he says, in front of everybody. "We haven't
had white rice for as long as I can remember!"

I think of my grandmother, her cooking, and our dinner
table.

Everybody wants to know what the boy is talking about.

"Do you have white rice every day, with every meal?" the
boy wants to know, not knowing when to stop.

I feel hot tears welling up in my eyes—from embarrass-
ment, from shame, or from sympathy, I don't know which.
I nod and turn away from him.

"I will make you a bow and some arrows one of these days," he says, following me, either ignoring or not comprehending the giggling going on among the other boys.

I keep on nodding my head, quickly walking away from him.

"I mean it," he says, trying to keep up with me.

I face him. "I know you mean it," I say. "Oh, come on! Do you want to race?" Before he can say anything, I am running as fast as I can toward the swings and the jungle gym at the far end of the field. "Come on!"

He gives out a joyful yelp and sprints after me. He knows he can run faster than I can—and I know that, too. In no time, he is running ahead of me, gleefully screaming, "I win! I win!"

. . . and now I am standing alone in front of the children of my class, watching them, waiting for our teachers to come out of the principal's office. "What a crowd," I think and marvel, looking around me at all the children—boys and girls, big ones and little ones: white shirts, blue shirts, brown shirts; white pants, black pants, brown pants, even green pants . . . round faces, square faces, long faces, flat faces, small faces . . . skinny bodies, chubby bodies . . . leather shoes, rubber shoes, sneakers, straw sandals . . . loud, quiet, sullen, cheerful, happy, miserable. . . . I am going to lose my name. They are going to lose their names. We are all going to lose our names. . . .

*   *   *

I am in the classroom with my teacher. With the shades half-drawn, it is dim inside, and the air is dank and musty. All the chairs are piled on top of the desks, and the wooden floor is spotless, having been washed, rinsed, waxed, and polished the day before the vacation began.

He is talking to me about the maps in the room. Although he is a Korean, he is speaking to me in Japanese, and I have to reply to him in Japanese. From the third grade up, we have been speaking Japanese at school and supposedly at home, too. Of course, all lessons are conducted in Japanese. We are not taught the Korean language or Korean history any longer. My father teaches me these subjects at home. We don't speak Japanese in our house.

The teacher says, "We must take down that map and put the new one up." He has brought a homemade map of the world, and he points his finger at a map that he and I put up the year before to replace an older one. He moves a desk against the wall, places a chair on top of the desk, and wants me to climb up on the chair to take down the old map. The new one is a world map that shows "who is with us and who is against us." It shows Japan, Germany, and Italy, and all their possessions, colonies, and recently annexed nations in one color—blue—and England, France, Russia, and most of the other countries in another color—red. America has no color—it is just a big white blank. The map has lots of arrows and lines drawn in blue and red, indicating which countries have what treaties, and so forth; for example, Germany, Italy, and Japan are linked by blue lines and arrows to indicate that they are the signatories of the Anti-Communist Treaty of November 6, 1937; it also records battles fought, countries and areas occupied, and so forth, for example, the battle on July 10, 1938, between Japanese and Russian troops, along the Mongolian-Manchurian border, an incident that has whipped the Japanese into an intense anti-Soviet Union, anti-Communist campaign throughout the Empire.

I pry thumbtacks from the wall and take down the map.

He takes it from me, tears it up, and throws it into a waste basket. He unrolls the new map and slides it up against the wall so I can thumbtack it on.

I jump down to the floor after I put the map on the wall. I look up at the map. It is nearly identical to the one he just threw into the waste basket.

He steps back a few paces. I stand by him.

"What do you think of the new map?" he asks.

I try to find words; I can read Japanese well, but I am not yet quick enough with Japanese words and sentences.

"Do you find something changed? Anything different?" he asks.

"Yes—I see changes." The Soviet Union now has a different color—green—and Germany and the Soviet Union are linked with a green line that runs through the Baltic Sea, connecting the two countries. In the middle of the Baltic Sea is a rectangular card that says, "German-Russian Mutual Non-aggression Treaty, August 23, 1939."

I ask him if this means that Germany and the Soviet Union are now allies and, therefore, that the Soviet Union is, also, an ally of Japan's now.

He does not answer for a moment. "I suppose you can say that," he says, at last, after gazing at the map, with a scowl on his face.

His voice does not convince me that I can really say that.

"I can tell you more about it later," he says, brushing off my further question, which deals with the battle between Japan and the Soviet Union along the Mongolian-Manchurian border. "I've just learned about this treaty myself," he says, "from the principal himself."

"Couldn't the principal explain it to the teachers, sir?"

"Of course, he could," he says; then, taking me by surprise: "Is your father in town now?"

"He is at the church," I say, puzzled as to why he would want to know about my father's whereabouts. A question like that does not portend anything good—for me, that is. "This is Sunday, you know, sir. Everyone in the family is at the church, except me, of course."

"Oh, I know that."

"Yes, sir."

"What I meant was," he says, rearranging the desk and the chair, "what he is going to be doing after the church."

"He is taking me down to the bookstore."

"Oh?"

"Yes, sir." There is only one bookstore in our town. My father is taking me there to tell the owner, who is a good friend of his, that, from now on, I will come in once a week and pick out a book of my choice in the store's children's book section; I am allowed to charge books to my father's account. I tell the teacher about it.

"You are a lucky boy," he says—rather enviously, I think.

"Yes, sir."

"When will you go down to the bookstore?" he asks. "I am going to be there myself, it so happens."

"After lunch, I imagine, sir," I say, picking up the waste basket, "that is, if you'd let me go home early, sir."

He gives me a funny look. "Empty that basket, and then you may go home. Give my regards to your father, will you?"

Ecstatic, I leap out of the room with the waste basket, which has a torn old map in it.

*   *   *

I tell my father about the teacher and his question and also about the new map, trying to explain as best I can about the Mutual Nonaggression Treaty between Germany and the Soviet Union. I ask him the same question I asked my teacher as to whether or not the Soviet Union is now to be considered Japan's ally. He, too, cannot answer that question, except to say that it is all very complicated and rather mysterious. "The teacher said he is going to go to the bookstore, too," I add, concluding my report.

My grandfather frowns and asks himself, "Now, what is he up to?"

My mother says quickly to me, "Run along now, and ask the maid for your lunch."

I move away from the grown-ups but not before I overhear my grandmother speaking to my father, "You'd better be careful with your words with him. He can't be trusted. He has always been a little sneaky since he was a boy, if you ask me."

My father says something about my teacher's being a little confused . . . and timid by nature. . . .

I giggle on the way to the kitchen, and I laugh hysterically once I am inside the kitchen, out of the grown-ups' range.

"Well, what are you so gleeful about?" asks the young maid, herself giggling for no good reason.

I look behind me and whisper to her, *"I've got a timid teacher!"*

"What? What?" she asks, though she is already laughing. "That's why you are home so early today?"

"Oh, you don't understand!" I announce. "There are certain things you girls do not understand."

She makes a face.

My little sister trots into the kitchen.

"You, too," I say, throwing up my arms.

"What did I do?" my sister asks. "Now, what did I do?"

"He thinks he's all grown up," says the maid. "Ha!"

I stride out of the kitchen, thinking that, suddenly, I do understand certain things, such as why my teacher wants to see my father, to meet him at the bookstore as if by chance, so that no one would think it strange. . . .

*   *   *

The bookstore is beside the graveled main street, a block or two from the open-air market place. The store is flanked, on the right, by a small restaurant with colorful dishes of noodles and fried fowls behind its dusty display windows and, on the left, by a doctor's office that has been opened recently by a young Korean doctor from Seoul. The store itself is spacious and is divided into a book section and a stationery section. I am going through the shelves of children's books, while my father is talking with the store owner and another friend of his. The store owner, a short man, leans against the counter, his elbows propped on it, his black hair falling on his pale, high-cheeked, bony face.

Once in a while, I look toward the door to see if my teacher is coming. I pause before a shelf containing adventure stories and pick out a book about the hunting of wild animals in Africa. Most of the books are written in Japanese. Only novels for adults—some of them, anyway—are in Korean. I am looking at pictures of animals, when the door opens and my teacher walks in. Standing by a magazine rack near the door, he nods to me. He leafs through a Japanese magazine, puts it down, picks up another, goes toward the counter with it. He bows to my father, his friend, and the store owner. There are, as it happens, no other people in the store.

The store owner says to my teacher, "The book you've ordered hasn't come in yet." He says this in Korean.

The other man, who also has a large apple orchard outside the town, says good-by to my father and walks away from the counter. He says, on his way out of the store, to me, "Be a good boy to your father now, hear!"—in Korean.

I go up to the counter, with the book. I bow to my teacher.

He wants to see my book. "It looks interesting," he says, in Korean, looking up from the black and white pictures of animals. "Do you enjoy reading books?"

"Yes, sir, I do," I reply in Japanese—out of habit. "My uncles in Tokyo send me books and magazines, sometimes, and I read them all."

He says, smiling, "It's all right for you to speak in Korean."

I look up at my father.

My father says, in Korean, "Why don't you look at some magazines over there? Maybe you can pick one up for your sister."

"Yes, sir"—in Korean. I know when I am dismissed. I move off to the children's magazine section.

"How is everything with you?" my father asks my teacher.
"How is the school work?"—in Korean.

The three of them are whispering now, and I can see my
father nod or shake his head once in a while. I can't hear
them too well, but I manage to catch a word or two . . .
"Poland" . . . "war" . . . "Nonaggression. . . ." My teacher
shakes his head, too, looking rather uncomfortable; then
he says, loud enough for me to hear, "Sometimes I don't
know what is going on in the world."

My father and the store owner exchange a glance, and my
father says, "We'll soon find out."

". . . We'll soon find out." . . . And we find out soon
enough what is going on in the world. A week later, on
September 1, 1939, Germany invades Poland, while the Soviet Union stands by watching, only to invade Poland a little
later to divide it up with Germany. Two days after the
German invasion of Poland, England and France declare
war against Germany; another two days later, America,
which everyone thought was an ally of England and France,
declares its neutrality, an occasion that causes my father to
brood all day and mutter to my mother, "I don't understand
this at all. Just what is going on?"

What is going on in the world? Even my father does not
know. We do not know what is happening in the world or
why, except that there is a war going on between the Japanese and the Chinese and there is another war going on in
Europe among all the powers—and Americans are watching,
sitting safely in that big white blank on our map, between
the Pacific and the Atlantic. . . .

My father beckons me to him and announces that we have
to go. I go up to the men and bow to them, bidding them
good-by.

My teacher says, "See you back in school soon." He turns
to my father. "When the school opens," he says, "even the

first- and second-graders won't be taught the Korean language and history, and I am afraid that's the end of any instruc-
tion in Korean."

"We knew it was coming to that," says the store owner.
"It was just a matter of when and how soon." His eyes
flash, taking in the store. "Look at it!" he says. "I see fewer
and fewer books in Korean, and you know that, pretty soon,
there won't be any book in our language being published."
He glares at my teacher. "Well, what the hell do you think of
that?" He shakes his finger at my teacher, as though my
teacher is largely to be blamed for his anguish. "You can't
even teach your own language and history to the children
of your own race. What the hell kind of a teacher are you
going to be anyway?"

"What can I do?" asks my teacher. "What can I do!"

"For one thing," says the store owner, "you can shape up
and start deciding just who you really are and what your
duties are to our children. I've been hearing a lot of disgraceful things about you lately and I don't care what you
think of me or what you can do to me, but you'd better keep
your eyes wide open and keep your wits about yourself."

"I don't know, sir," says my teacher. "I just don't know."

I am quietly standing by them, trying to look as incon-
spicuous as I can and, watching my teacher suddenly shrink-
ing, as it were, in stature and manliness in the presence
of the two men—the two most illustrious members of the
small elite in town who have been to college—I, somehow,
begin to feel a little sorry for him—presumptuously enough—
and, also, begin to think that I can understand his problems,
whatever they may really be. The bookstore owner went to
a college in Seoul, as did most of his regular customers (his
friends). My teacher graduated from a normal school in our
province, a public school whose students are subsidized by
the Japanese.

The store owner is saying, "Just because the Japanese paid

for you to go to a normal school doesn't mean you have to sell your soul to them and become their slave."

"Those are strong words, sir," says my teacher. "I am not that rotten."

"Look here, you two," says my father, drawing me near to him, putting his arm around my shoulders, as if to remind them of my presence. I try to look innocent and small, pretending to be absorbed in the pictures of lions and elephants in Africa. "Patience," he says.

"Patience! Patience, indeed!" says the store owner.

"I am beginning to see a certain pattern emerging from the world situation," says my father, in a tone of voice that reminds me of my maternal grandfather, who is a minister in Pyongyang. "It will become clearer very soon, and, meanwhile, we should be quiet and look for a revelation, if you know what I mean." His words and his tone make me think again of my grandfather when he prays, not with his entire congregation in the church but with a small group of his friends at home.

"You are right, sir," says my teacher to my father.

"But—oh, how long!" says the store owner. "How long!"

"It won't be long," says my father firmly and, I think, rather cryptically.

After that, no one says anything for a while.

Patience . . . patience. Lord, how long, oh, how long? Someone asked that in the Bible, and there was no answer, or was there?

We all part in silence. At the door, I bow to my teacher and bid him good-by once more.

He bends down a little, puts his hand on my head, and, abruptly, pulls me to him, with his arm around my shoulders.

Startled, I look up.

He mumbles a word or two to my father and walks out of the store.

"Come," says my father. "We must get back to the orchard."

With my new book and a magazine for my sister in hand, I follow him outside into the hazy afternoon sun.

My teacher walks across the dusty street, dodging a row of rattling, jingling oxcarts, and disappears into a shadowy alley by a hardware store and a grain store.

"Father," I say, when I can't see my teacher any longer, "the teacher was crying."

He nods but does not say anything while we walk through the open-air market place, which is now deserted, cross an intersection, and march past a row of Japanese-owned department stores, restaurants, and other shops. He says, "I am sure he was not crying for you."

"What do you mean, sir?"

"Let's hope he was crying for himself," he says, looking straight ahead. "It is a small beginning."

I do not understand his words, though I sense they are "significant," because my father speaks them in such a grave tone of voice, which suggests he is speaking to himself more than to others, even me.

I follow him in silence, feeling important and secretive. For I know that, either by chance or by design, I was allowed the rare distinction of being with the three men while they were engaged in what the grown-ups call a "dangerous" conversation, and that I saw inexplicable tears in the eyes of my teacher—this sight is, for me, a somber and overwhelming secret that I resolve not to tell my friends, mere children. I quicken my pace and stride down the street, which is shimmering in the blazing hot afternoon sun, holding my head high, following my father's steps.

*   *   *

Today, unlike on other Sundays, we stay for dinner with my grandparents and start back to the orchard in the early evening. My father gives his bicycle to the oxcart driver and tells him to go on ahead of us to the orchard, so that he can be with his family for dinner. "The moon will be out," my father says to him, "and we will be all right. Don't wait up for us." My father is going to drive the oxcart.

Before dinner, I help feed our oxen, helping another tenant farmer who lives in small quarters by the west gate. He is young and unmarried, and helps around the main house, doing odd jobs but, mainly, taking care of the oxen and carts. Near the stall, he has a big open-air kitchen with enormous iron kettles for boiling beans and other feed for the oxen. With a big shovel, he spoons the cooked green beans, husks and stalks and all, into wooden troughs, while, with a pump, I fill other troughs with water from the well nearby. It is dusk, and the air is hazy and smoky from the smoldering fire in the kitchen. The farmer gives me beans still in their husks, which he has cooked by burying them in hot ashes. I crack the husks and eat the beans, savoring the warm, smoky taste. He likes to teach me all sorts of tricks —how to trap squirrels, so that I can keep them in a big cage he helped me make, which has a couple of wheels inside that the squirrels can ride on, or how to catch sparrows, which get fat and delicious in the fall, after harvest time. To catch sparrows, we set up a large bamboo basket on a piece of stick and tie a long string to the stick and hide in the farmer's room; then, when sparrows come directly under the basket to eat the grain we have sprinkled there, we pull the string and trap the sparrows inside the basket. He then covers the basket with a big sheet, puts his hand inside the basket and catches the birds. He sends me away for a few minutes, saying that I am still too little to watch him and learn what to do after we catch the sparrows. I come back when he calls me—and he has the birds in a skewer, already cooked in the fire. . . . The young farmer wants to get married, and he is looking for a girl. When he finds a girl, he will tell my father about her and her family, and my father will begin negotiating with her parents as to the terms of the marriage, and, eventually, the farmer and his bride will get free, from my father, a house near the orchard and money to start their new life. When they have a baby, they will get free, from my father, a piece of farm land, and, when their children are big enough to go to school, my father will pay for their schooling. The village by our orchard is settled by farmers who have worked for my father and who are still working for him, even after they have their own families. Standing outside the stall, watching the big oxen munching on the beans, the young farmer and I are sharing the cooked beans, and, emboldened by a sense of camaraderie, I dare ask him, "Have you found a girl yet?"

He gives out a great big guffaw, rolling his eyes heavenward. "If your mother could just hear you!" Then, in a conspiratorial hush, he says, "I've found two girls, and I'll let you know which one I will marry when I decide which one I like better."

I nod, wisely. "I won't tell my father about the two girls. Not yet anyway."

"That's a good boy. No need to rush, right?"

"Anyone I know?"

"Sure."

"Who?"

He looks at me with sly, amused eyes. "Next time I come out to the orchard, you just keep your eyes on me and you'll know."

"All right."

"You'd better run along now," he says, wiping his mouth with his sleeve. "You'd better go get your supper."

"All right." I wipe my mouth with my sleeve.

"Hey, don't do that!" he says. "Where's your handkerchief?"

I pat my pants pocket and run off, laughing.

"Your mother will have a fit!" he shouts after me, laughing.

"I won't tell anyone about your two girls!" I shout back.

"Hey! hey! not so loud, not so loud, will you!"

I laugh all the way back to the main house, panting with joy.

*   *   *

The big, bright round moon is floating peacefully in the cloudless night sky. I sit by my father, who drives the ox-cart, and I watch the shadows of the ox and ourselves creeping along on the road. The hulking body of the ox sways as it pulls the cart slowly, jingling the big brass bell on its neck. My mother sits in the back with my sister, who is asleep. We do not speak, listening to the symphony of chirpings vibrating the night air all around us. Jingling, jingling, chirping, chirping . . . and it is cool and peaceful, and it seems to me that my friends, my teacher, the school, the town—everything—belong to another world and another time. Out of town and in the middle of shadowy, moonlit plains and hills, with no one else in sight and with the twinkling of yellowish lights from the farmhouses and huts studded here and there in the dark hills, I breathe in the comforting presence of my father, my mother, and my little sister, serenely content and secure, joyfully aware of their nearness, unafraid of the dark, the unknown, and the world beyond the plains and the hills . . . and oblivious of the war. My world then is small and private and secure—and I nestle against my father, knowing that he will safely lead us back to our cottage in the peaceful, glorious, and happy orchard. . . .

There is a light tap on my shoulder. I wake up. "We are home," says my father. His arm is around my shoulders. I look back. My sister is still asleep, with her head on my mother's lap. The oxcart jingles and creaks its way by the farmhouses. There are people outside, sitting on straw mats on the ground in front of their houses. Men smoking pipes are gathered around a pot of incense. I see the red glow of their pipes and the hazy smoke curling up

in the cool, bright night air. They get up as we pass by and
bow to my father, greeting him with pleasantries. I wave
at them. Ahead of us, a young farmer stands by the orchard's
gate with a kerosene lantern. Fireflies are swarming in the
bush by the gate, and I think I might catch them tomorrow
night, perhaps, and put them in a paper lantern. Inside
the gate, we get down from the cart. My father takes my
sister from my mother and carries the girl in his arms. The
farmer will take the ox and the cart to the stall. The back
of my father's white shirt is bright in the moonlight as he
walks up the knoll toward the cottage. My mother takes my
hand, and, together, we follow my father. Soft, yellowish
light shines from inside the cottage, and the farmer's young
wife comes down the path and greets us. Half of the cottage
is in the thick, black shadows of the towering trees, and the
other half is bathed in the moonlight. I linger outside
awhile, taking in the tranquil expanse of the orchard, listening to the familiar chirpings of crickets and inhaling the
cool, clean air.

The mountains and hills surrounding the orchard, in the
shadows, seem taller and more awesome, almost brooding.
I look up and see millions of stars and the moon serenely,
almost indifferently, gazing down. Suddenly, I think of the
maps, with ever changing colors and arrows and lines, with
victors and conquerors and the vanquished and the captive,
thumbtacked on the wall of our classroom, and it strikes me
that the maps ought to show those millions of stars and the
moon and the sun, too—all those things that never change
and that are always up there in the sky. A silly thought
makes me almost laugh out loud: Those who make maps
are not aware of the sun, the moon, and the stars because
they never bother to look up. I look up—and I am struck
by another silly thought: If someone up there is drawing a
map, and if he, too, never bothers to look up from his map
and down to the earth, then his map won't show the earth—

or, even if he does look toward the earth, the earth will be simply a tiny dot or, at best, a little star. . . .

Gazing up at the dark heaven swirling with millions of twinkling stars makes me dizzy. I look down, once again surveying the dark orchard, the fireflies in the bush, and the soft glow inside the cottage—and I look up heavenward once more—and, for some strange reason, I am suddenly afraid of the night sky, the awesome immensity of the celestial world above, and the omnipresent dark shadows. I run into the cottage.

"Go to bed now," my mother says. "You can sleep as late as you want tomorrow morning."

My father rumples my hair. "Good night," he says. "You had a long day."

"Yes, sir. Good night."

In bed, I lie awake for a long time, remembering the day. I think about the tears in my teacher's eyes, and my father's words. My teacher "crying for himself." "A small beginning." I do not understand these words fully, but I keep thinking and thinking about the tears in his eyes when he impulsively pulled me to him. I think of the words of the bookstore owner, too: "Start thinking about yourself. . . what you really are." Does an act of thinking about oneself—to know what one really is—make one sorrowful and bring tears to one's eyes? I think of the way I giggled and announced to the maid that I had a "timid teacher," and how we laughed about it. My mind wanders, and I think about the cold, dark heaven and the black shadows on the earth, and I think of the strange fright that drove me into the cottage . . . and tears well up in my eyes and slide down my cheeks. I do not know why I am crying. I merely think—again and again—of the tears in my teacher's eyes and of the terrifying infinity of the night sky.

My mother is standing by my bed. "What's the matter," she whispers. "Why are you crying?"

"I don't know, Mother."

"Did you have a bad dream? A nightmare?"

"I don't know."

"You must be tired. Don't be afraid of bad dreams. They are just bad dreams, that's all. We are here, you know. Go to sleep."

"Yes."

She holds my hand, for a while, quietly. I hear the rustling of papers in the other room where I know my father is reading a newspaper. I feel limp and very tired and, closing my eyes slowly, taking in the luminous silhouette of my mother drawing the curtains by the moonlit window, I drift into sleep.

Lost Names

It is February, the gloomiest and the cruelest time of the interminable winter in our northern region. The sun seldom ventures out in the dark heaven, as if it, too, finds repugnant the dreary sky, ever shrouded with impenetrable dirty grayness that tenaciously, almost perversely, defies the light and its warmth.

And it snows and snows and snows—not the silvery, glittering, fluffy flakes that descend from a clear sky, dancing and gliding like millions of white flower petals blowing in the wind, but the wet, heavy, dull things that pelt down from a soiled sky, deepening the snow on the ground, which is already knee-deep, and instantly hardening into a brittle, treacherous sheet of ice. There is nothing you can do. You can't go down to the river to skate with your friends on a rink you have shoveled out, because the snow is coming down constantly, and, even if you cleared the snow off the rink for a little while, the surface of the frozen river is too rough and jagged, and then it will be quickly covered up

again by the relentless snow anyway. You can't even make
a snowman out of this kind of snow; it is like frozen glass,
and it will break into hundreds of razor-sharp pieces the
moment you step on it or shovel into it.

People are driven into the cold, dank, and gray recesses of
their houses with nothing much to do but to think about
the warm spring, the hot, yet exhilarating, summer, and the
glorious fall—and about the end of the winter when at last
the wind will stop howling in the dead of the night and your
ears will feel, suddenly, a faint touch of warmth from somewhere and, one morning, perhaps, you will find, by chance,
a tiny bud that is miraculously green with life. Children are
bound, too, into wherever they can find a little warmth,
with a monotonous routine and a frustrating and demoralizing suspicion that, somehow, life has come to a stop. But,
of course, life has not come to an end; it is, simply, in cap-
tivity, in the grips of a very cruel season. . . .

It is morning—gray, as usual, and snowing madly, as
usual. I am standing on the veranda outside my room; in
the winter, the veranda is enclosed with sliding glass doors;
I am watching the new young tenant farmer who is trying
to make a footpath through the courtyard to the east gate.
He has taken the place of the other farmer, who got married
in the fall and now lives out by the orchard with his wife.
The courtyard is covered with deep snow, as hard and rough
as ice, and the farmer is pounding on the icy snow with a
big hoe, breaking it up first, then scooping up the jagged
chunks with a shovel. He will then use his hoe again to dig
deeper into the old layers of snow, which is now really a
bed of ice. The flower beds are gone, invisible under the
snow, and the stone walks are buried under, too, and the
evergreens are drooping and stooping low, heavily laden with
frozen snow. The young farmer is now putting strips of
straw matting on the path, but the snow is coming down
ferociously, and it quickly covers up the mats.

I press my face against the thickly frosted windowpane,

watching his white breath puffing and puffing as he bends down, laying thick planks of wood on top of the straw mats. He stretches up and acknowledges my presence with a toss of his snow-covered head. I wave. He waves back, then he looks up, letting his face be pelted by the snow, shaking his fists at the sky. He looks at me with a grin and goes back to his quarters, walking across the courtyard, his legs sinking up to the knees, his boots gouging out big, deep cracks in the snow. The snow seems to be coming down harder, wildly, as if its big flakes have gone "berserk," as my grandmother would say, swirling and zigzagging, clashing with each other, shooting down in every haphazard way.

My sister tiptoes out to the veranda, all bundled up in a pink quilt which she drags behind her. She is barefoot, and, because the floor is cold, she walks on her heels, tottering and waddling like a little penguin, and comes beside me.

"What are you doing?" she says.

"Nothing."

"Cold!" She touches her nose to the windowpane. "Snowing, snowing all the time!"

"It will stop someday," I say, though without conviction.

"Father says to come in and have breakfast."

"All right."

"Are you going to skate today?"

"Are you kidding? I haven't skated for days and days!"

"I miss Mother."

"What's that got to do with skating?"

"I don't know. I just wondered about what Mother is doing right now."

My mother is away in Pyongyang, an hour's train ride north from our town, to be with her parents, and, of course, our new baby is away, too—my new baby sister.

"Feeding the baby, probably," I say, knowingly. "What else?"

My sister makes a face. She is almost six, and, to my surprise, she has been friendlier to me since the arrival of the baby, who turned out to be a girl, to my disappointment. She scratches the frosted windowpane with her fingernails, drawing a big circle. She gives it three strands of "hair" at the top, chisels in two round eyes and a wide circle for a mouth, then she mimics—"Waah, Waah!"

"What's that supposed to mean?" I say.

"They can keep the baby as long as they want, but I want my mother back. Waah, Waah!"

"Oh, come on. She is your sister, you know, after all."

"And yours, too. Big deal."

"Oh, come on."

"I wish I had a baby brother."

Wisely, I admonish her. "You don't know what you are talking about."

She blows her breath furiously against her etching on the windowpane and melts it away, scratching at it with her fingernails at the same time. "Would you make a pair of skates for me?"

"You can't even skate," I say casually.

"Will you teach me how?"

"You don't even have skates." The moment I say that, I know I am trapped.

"That's why I asked you to make me a pair."

She is too smart for me. "I don't know how to make them."

"You do, too. You made some for yourself. You are very clever; do you know that?"

"Well, Father helped me," I admit reluctantly. "Why don't you ask Father?"

"Because . . ."

"Because what?"

"Because . . . if I ask you, you would ask Father to help you make a pair for me, then he will help you make a pair for me and then . . ."

I stop her there; I know I have to give in to her sooner or later. "You've got to get a piece of iron and take it down to a blacksmith, and he will melt it down and hammer on it and make blades."

She can't be bothered with the details. She is scratching on the windowpane again, drawing a skate.

"Then you nail the blades on pieces of wooden board and you hammer in ten or maybe twelve nails on each side of the board so you can lace a string over your boots, and that's all there is to it."

"Well, will you make me a pair?" She has drawn a long blade, which curls up in the front, like the bow of an ancient Viking ship.

"Go ask Father. I am going to have my breakfast."

No sooner do I take a step away from her than she says, "Wait till Mother comes back. I'll tell her all about it."

I whirl around. "Tell her what?"

"Nothing."

"Tell her what!"

She huddles up into the quilt, as if she is expecting a blow from me. "You'd better be nice to me and make me a pair of skates," she squeaks.

"You'll tell Mother what?"

"Well, you know, that you've let Grandmother pack your lunch box with white rice and eggs and meat and something like that."

I am stunned and hurt. "Don't you dare! That's not fair! Besides, it's not my fault. It's Grandmother's fault, not mine!"

"Well . . ."

I am in fury and shame. "You don't have to wait till Mother comes back. I'll show you right now!"

I give her a shove and march across the veranda to the kitchen. My grandmother, as usual, is in there, "helping" the maid. I hold the kitchen door open a second and, without daring to look at my grandmother, say loudly and firmly:

"I don't want white rice in my lunch box ever!"

I slam the door shut and run back to my room before anyone can say a word. In my room, I dump out all the books and notebooks and pencils from my school bag and put them back in again one by one. I open the drawers of my desk and rummage through all the things in them, looking for something without knowing what. I am afraid of starting to cry. . . .

I do not know how much time has passed when my father comes into my room. I pretend not to notice him.

"Come and have breakfast," he says. "You don't want to be late for school."

I am sitting at my desk, not looking up.

"That is enough now," he says.

I do not respond.

I understand the way you feel about your lunch," he says. "Come on now."

I get up and turn to face him, and, at that moment, I lose control and begin to sob. My words come out muffled and incoherent even to me. "I don't want to have white rice in my lunch box, sir," I am saying. "Most of my class-mates don't ever have white rice in their lunch boxes and some of them always want to taste it and if I don't let them they make fun of me, like saying just because I am a rich boy and so on, and I've had my lunch box stolen, I mean, someone ate my lunch while I was out of the room, and that happened three, four times already and . . ."

"Why haven't you told us about it?" he says. "You haven't said anything about someone stealing your lunch. What did you do when you found your lunch box was empty?"

"It was never empty, because whoever stole it put his lunch in it instead; I mean, sir, with barley or millet."

"I see."

"I want Mother home, sir."

"She will be home in a few days."

"Well, she's been gone for a long time."

"She's been gone only for a week or so."

"If she's home and if she packs my lunch box, you know she won't pack it with white rice."

"I know. That's your mother. That's like her."

"I know that, sir. And that's what I mean, sir. Grandmother insists on . . ."

"That's your grandmother, you know," he says, putting his arm around my shoulders. "And that's very much like your grandmother. She just wants you to have the best thing."

"Well, sir, I don't want white rice in my lunch box. That's all, sir. It is not the best thing for me."

"I understand that. You feel uncomfortable eating white rice when most of your friends are eating barley and millet, that's it, isn't it?"

I nod. "It makes me feel as if I am showing off and things like that."

He gives my shoulders a tight squeeze. "It's like with your skates, isn't it?"

"Yes, sir." I have a pair of skates with real leather shoes and shiny steel blades, made in Canada, a present from some missionary friends in Manchuria. Few children in my class have real skates. Most of them make their own. After my first day at the rink on the river, I came home, determined to make my own skates, too. My father caught me when I was scrounging around in the storeroom, looking for a piece of iron or steel, which I wanted to take down to a blacksmith.

"Well, let's see what we can do about the rice," says my father, leading me out of the room. "I'll talk with your grandmother about it and I am sure she'll understand. But I want you to promise me to be gentle with her."

"Yes, sir. I do understand how she feels about my lunch."

"Of course, you do. You know how much she enjoys cooking for us, but since last fall—well, you know what I mean."

I nod, suddenly feeling a little sad for my old grand-mother.

In our storeroom, we have always had several big jars, as tall as I am, filled with white rice, but, since last fall, there is only half a jar of white rice, and the others are filled with barley, rye, and millet. White rice is scarce and expensive, not because the rice harvest is poor but because, now, our rice farmers are forced by law to sell their rice to the government at a cut-rate price; rice is then shipped to Japan (which the Japanese want us to call the "mainland"), leaving very little rice in Korea. Now, only the Japanese and very rich Koreans can afford white rice. We have been eating rice mixed, mostly, with millet or, sometimes, with corn or barley. Only when it is someone's birthday or when a guest comes do we get to have white rice with beef or chicken. Meat and fowl are also bought up by the Japanese, through a process they call a "voluntary contribution to the national war effort for the glory of the Emperor" and are shipped to the "mainland." "They want us to starve to death or to get sick and die of undernourishment, which is the same thing," declares my grandmother, when she and my mother are putting rice in small paper bags—to make sure we have one bag of rice a day, mixed with other grains. She now has very little cooking to do. . . . She insists that the children should have white rice and meat and an egg, once in a while, for their health—"even if we have to sell everything we have" —but my mother won't hear of it. "If we have to suffer hard-ship, Mother," says my mother, "then we must suffer to-gether. Besides, we are still much better off than others who have no rice at all, and I know that most of the school children never get to have rice."

My mother is away in Pyongyang with her parents, how-ever, and my grandmother is cheerfully taking advantage of her absence; she "informs" my father that I, at least, should have white rice and meat or an egg for my lunch. "A boy growing up," says she, "ought to eat well. Besides, if I can't

take care of the feeding of my grandchildren, what else am
I good for." My father gives in to her, after extracting a
promise from her that, as soon as my mother comes back, she
will let "the boy's mother" handle the lunch. My grandmother says, with tears in her eyes, "Your grandfather and
I have slaved our way up to where we are so our children
and grandchildren and their children will live better than
we have." To her, who lived in poverty and ignorance in
her childhood and most of her youth, living "better" means
simply living in a house with a tiled roof and having white
rice rather than barley or millet and having meat and
chicken and eggs—in short, eating well and not worrying
about where one's meals are going to come from for the next
day. "And look what happens!" she says. "We have rice,
meat, chicken, everything we need, and, yet, we can't have
any of them. How am I supposed to feel? The Japanese taking everything from us, so their children can have everything, while our own children are going around hungry and
undernourished. How am I supposed to feel about that?"
The intricacies and complexities of politics and economics
matter very little to her. "Damn them," she says. "They just
want to fatten up their children, so they can make soldiers
out of them faster, so they can go out and pester people like
us." She does not understand that farmers are no longer
raising cattle, pigs, or chickens, because they know that they
will be "requisitioned" at a very low price by the Japanese,
and the same is true with rice. Rather than see their produce
requisitioned and shipped off to Japan, many farmers have
simply stopped farming and grow only "just enough to live
on." The Japanese are requisitioning everything, even our
apples.

   At breakfast, which I have with my father and sister, my
sister says she is sorry for her "nasty behavior," and I accept
her apology with magnanimity. I am late for school; so I
rush through the breakfast—rice mixed with millet, half and
half; potato soup; and pickles. I go to the kitchen to get my

lunch box. My grandmother says, without looking at me, "Your lunch box is by the oven." She has put it there to keep it warm until I am ready to leave for school. I pick it up and put it in the book bag. I don't know what to say to her. I inch my way toward the door, trying to think of words. "I am sorry I fussed," I am finally able to say. She is stooped down, tending the fire in the oven, stirring up embers and hot ashes with a stick. She doesn't turn around. The young maid signals to me to speak to her again. I go near her, stand behind her, and say, "Grandmother, I am sorry I made such a fuss about the lunch." She straightens up, with her hand on her hip. "Oh, it's you." I nod. "Are your shoes dry?" I nod again. "Warm enough?" "Yes." "Gloves?" I take them out of a coat pocket to show her. "I have to take them off at the school gate," I say.

. . . Wearing gloves is forbidden at the school; keeping our hands in our pants pockets is forbidden, too; we have the pants pockets and jacket pockets all sewn up—the school regulation—"keeping your hands in pockets harms your posture and weakens your constitution, resulting in your becoming weak men, unfit to serve the Imperial Cause . . ." and so forth. When my mother sewed up my pockets, she shook her head and said, "Why not, then, make the school uniform without any pockets in the first place?" We have to buy our uniforms at the school store. My father said, "Think about the state of mind behind this sort of thing." He has a habit of saying things that are too enigmatic for me to comprehend, such as, "It is surrealistic," when I told him that each child in the school was required to make his own wooden rifle, which was to be carved out of a piece of wood, for the school's "armory." He enjoyed that occasion, helping me out, saying, "What about a wooden bayonet, too?" "It is the beginning of the end," he said to my mother who simply shook her head. . . .

"Good-by, Grandmother," I say.

"Wait a second," she says and directs the maid to bring

her a sheet of old newspaper. She digs out a sweet potato from under hot ashes in the oven, scrubs the ashes off the fist-sized potato and wraps it up with the newspaper. "Here," she says, "it tastes good. Maybe you can warm it up on the stove in your classroom, if you don't eat it now. And you can keep your hands warm with it, on your way."

"Thank you, Grandmother." The potato is still sizzling inside the newspaper. I smell the smoked sweetness mixed with the inky odor of the newspaper.

"Well, go on now," she says. "I'll have some buckwheat pancakes for you when you come home." Ah—Grandmother!

I bound out of the steamy, smoky, warm kitchen into the bitter cold air, curling my fingers around the toasty warmth of the sweet potato.

The young farmer is shoveling the snow by the east gate. I say, "Good morning" to him as I dash through the gate.

"Hey!" he calls after me. "You forgot these."

He is coming toward me with three pieces of firewood tied up with a straw rope.

I take the logs from him. "Thank you." We are required to bring two logs or a sack of pine cones for the stove in our classroom. In the fall and before the snow starts, we often, instead of doing schoolwork, are sent up to the hills and mountains to collect pine cones, which are then stored in our classroom for the long winter. Coal is scarce, and what little coal we get from the school's warehouse is not enough to keep our single potbellied stove going through the winter. So we burn the coal mixed with pine cones, and, when the supply runs out, we must bring either firewood or pine cones on our own; two logs or a sack of pine cones; as the class leader, I am asked to contribute more—three logs three times a week. Other children contribute twice a week. There is one advantage in assuming an extra burden: I get to sit next to the stove—to keep an eye on it and make sure the fire is kept going—and to have my lunch box placed right on top of the stove just before lunch time comes around. Other children pile their tin lunch boxes over mine to warm them up. The second place, that is, the right to place one's lunch box over mine on the stove, is given to anyone who stays after school to help me clean up the stove and have it ready for the next day.

With my book bag and the steaming sweet potato in one hand and three logs in the other, I fight my way through the snow and the howling wind to the school, soon joined by a long line of children, each carrying logs or a sack of pine cones.

But, after all, there is no school that morning—for me and a few other children, that is. When I arrive at the school, our teacher is already in our classroom. He is a young Japanese, a recent graduate of a college in Tokyo. He is twenty-four years old, soft-spoken, and rather gentle with the children. He is lean, in fact, so lean that we give him a nickname the moment he is assigned to our class: Chopstick. Always pale-faced and looking in poor health, he likes to recite Japanese poetry in class, though we hardly understand it.

I set about making the fire in the stove, with the help of several of my friends, who will later toss a coin to see who gets the "second place." The air in the classroom is freezing and, through my cotton socks, I can feel the icy chill of the wooden floor. It is unusual for our teacher to be in the classroom before the bell rings, so all the children are silent, hunched over their desks, rubbing their feet furtively to keep them warm. The teacher is sitting on his chair, behind the lectern on the platform, quietly looking at us. When I have the fire going at last, I shovel in some coal on top of the pine cones crackling inside the blazing stove. The stove sits in the middle of a square, tin floorboard in the center of the class. It is like a small island. I sit at a desk next to it, checking it regularly or adding more water to a tea kettle sizzling on top of it.

The bell rings, and we sit up straight, hushed.

The teacher stands up, looking at a piece of paper in his bony hand. He keeps silent for a long time, looking out the windows. It is almost like a blizzard outside—the wind roaring and howling, the snow whipping down, slanting at nearly a forty-five–degree angle. The snow is so heavy and thick that I can barely make out the other buildings across the frozen pond.

"Well," he says.

And I bid the children rise from their chairs, and, when they do, I command them to bow to our teacher. We all bow our heads to him; then we sit down.

"Today," he says, without looking at us, holding up the piece of paper in front of him, "I must have your new names. I have the new names of most of you in this class, but the principal tells me that some of you have not yet registered your names. I shall call your old names, and those who are called will be excused from the class immediately, so that they can go home and return with their new names, which have been properly registered with the proper authorities in town. Do you understand what I am saying?"

Without waiting for our reaction, and still without looking at us, he calls out several names. My name is called.

"You may be excused," he says, crunching the piece of paper into a ball in his fist. "Report back as soon as you can."

He gets down from the platform and says, "The rest of you will remain quiet and go over your homework." With that announcement, he abruptly turns away from us and walks out of the room.

I put my shoes on outside the classroom and, brushing aside the questions from the bewildered children, I start running away from the school as fast as I can in the blinding snow and choking, icy wind, running and skidding and stumbling in the deep snow. My new name, my old name, my true name, my not-true name? I am plunging and slogging through the snow, thinking, "I am going to lose my

name; I am going to lose my name; we are all going to lose
our names." . . .

*   *   *

My grandmother says, "Leave the boy home. He will
catch cold."

My father says, "No, Mother. I want him to come with me.
I want him to see it and remember it." My father is wearing a Korean man's clothes: white pantaloon-like trousers,
with the bottoms tied around his ankles, a long-sleeved
white jacket, a blue vest, and a gray topcoat. My father is
seldom seen in our native clothes, except when he has to attend a wedding or a funeral. He is wearing a black armband
on the left sleeve of his gray topcoat. He is not wearing a hat.

"Have some hot soup before you go," says my grandmother.

"No, thank you, Mother," says my father, holding my
hand. "Stay with Father and keep an eye on him."

My grandmother nods. "It is the end of the world," she
mutters angrily. "Damn them! damn them!"

"Come on," says my father to me.

Outside, by the west gate, four of my father's friends are
waiting for us. They are dressed like my father—all wearing
black armbands on the left sleeves of their gray topcoats.
I bow to them, but no one says a word either to me or to
anyone else. On the small stone bridge outside the gate,
they pause for a moment, whispering among themselves. The
stream is frozen and covered thick with snow. Passers-by bow
to the group. The four men—my father's friends—are the
bookstore owner, an elder of our Presbyterian church, a
doctor, and a farmer who also has an apple orchard. The
snow is slashing down on us, and my ears are cold, even with
ear muffs on. Snowflakes get inside my collar, making me
shiver. We walk down the street; my father is in the middle
of the group, holding my hand. I slip on an icy patch and

stumble, and the bookstore owner helps me up and holds my hand. In the snow-covered open-air market place, which is closed down during the winter, the wind howls even more strongly, shrieking through the electric wires and telephone poles. The snow is beating down so hard that I have to bow my head and face sideways, but the men are walking straight up, occasionally returning, in silence, the bows from the other men on the street. We go past the town hall, past the Japanese department store and shops, and through the main street, where most of the shops are—the bakery, the barber shop, the watch shop, the restaurant, the clothing store, the bicycle shop, the grain store, the pharmacy, the doctor's office, the dentist's office, the hardware store, the bank, the grocery store . . . and the townspeople are looking out from their shops and offices—some bowing to us, some waving at us—and, as we continue down the main street, we are followed by other people, and more and more people join us as we come near the end of the main street. My father and the bookstore owner are still holding my hands, and I have to try hard to keep up with the men, though they are walking very slowly. At the end of the main street, we come to an intersection and turn to the right. It is an uphill road, and the snow-laden wind whips down from the top of the hill, almost blowing me off my feet, and I feel the men's hands tighten their grips on mine. At the top of the hill, there is a small Methodist church and, across from it, the police station. We struggle up the snow-packed hill, by the long stone wall of the police station, and enter its main gate. Inside, on the station grounds, in the deep snow, a long line of people barely moves along. We walk over the crackling snow and stand at the end of the line. We exchange bows with the people standing in line. No one says anything—I, my father, the bookstore owner, the doctor, the farmer, the elder of our church, and all those people who have preceded or followed us . . .

I am freezing with cold. I stamp my feet, crushing the icy

snow on the ground. Without a word, the bookstore owner opens the front of his topcoat and pulls me inside and covers me up, except for my face, which is snuggled against the back of my father. He turns, looks at me, and fixes my ear muffs. He neither says a word to me nor smiles at me. I know when to keep quiet.

The line, hardly advancing, gets longer and longer. New people are lined up even outside the station grounds.

Someone comes to us. Someone from the front of the line. He is a young Korean man. He bows to my father. "Please, sir," he says, "come and take my place."

My father shakes his head. "I will wait for my turn here. Thank you anyway."

He stands silent for a moment.

"It is all right," my father says. "Go back to your place."

He bows to my father once more and says, before he returns to the front of the line, "I am dying of shame, sir"; then, his words nearly lost in the howling snow, "I don't know what I can do."

A little while later, a Japanese policeman comes toward us. When he comes near to us, I can tell that he is an inspector. He is wearing a black cape. I see his long saber peering out of the bottom of his cape. I can hear the clank the saber makes against his black leather riding boots. He salutes my father. He has a long turned-up mustache. "It is an honor," he says to my father, "to see you in person here. You could have sent one of your servants."

My father is silent.

"Please come with me," says the Inspector. "I can't have you lined up out here like a common person. Please."

"I will wait for my turn, just like everyone else," says my father. "They have been here longer than I have."

"Come with me," insists the Inspector. "Please."

Afraid and, to my shame, trembling, I look up at my father.

My father looks at the Inspector and then at his friends. Other people are watching us.

I feel the hands of the bookstore owner tighten on my shoulders.

"If you insist," says my father.

The Inspector looks down at me. "You must be freezing," he says. His white-gloved hand reaches out for my snow-covered hair.

I duck my head inside the topcoat of the bookstore owner.

"Bring the boy with you, by all means," says the Inspector.

I hear my father's boots crunching on the snow. I free myself out of the bookstore owner's hands and nearly bump into the back of my father.

He takes my hand. "Come with me."

The Inspector walks beside my father. His black cape is billowing in the wind and snow, flapping and flapping— and his saber jingling and clanking. We walk toward the front door of the granite station building. As we pass by the people in the line, they bow to my father silently. My father's head is bowed, and, without looking at the people, he goes slowly, holding my hand.

The Inspector opens the front door and holds it for us. A Korean detective inside the building quickly bows to my father. "You really didn't have to come in person, sir," he says in Korean. "I would have been glad to have registered your new name for you if I had known you were coming in person. In this cold."

We are inside the station. Other people in the line are admitted inside one at a time. The air is steamy and warm. The hallway is swarming with black-uniformed policemen, all wearing sabers. The wooden floor is slushy with melting snow.

The Inspector ushers us into a large room immediately to the right of the hallway by the door. There are two big tables, each with a policeman sitting behind. At each table, by the side of the Japanese policeman, a Korean detective sits on a chair, apparently interpreting for those Koreans who cannot understand Japanese.

The Korean detective who met us at the door brings a chair from the back of the room. He offers it to my father.

My father does not sit down.

The Inspector tells the detective to bring some tea.

One of the men sitting at one of the tables facing the Japanese policeman cannot speak Japanese and has to have the words interpreted. The man is old; he helps out in the open-air market place on market days, doing odd jobs.

The Japanese policeman, dipping a pen in an inkwell, does not lift his face from a large ledger on the table when he says to the Korean detective by his side, "Tell the old man we will pick out a name for him if he can't make up his mind."

The Korean detective picks up a sheet of paper and shows it to the old man, translating the policeman's words.

The old man shakes his head, looking at the paper, which contains a long list of names. "Anything," he mumbles. "It doesn't matter."

The Korean detective does not translate those words. Instead, he puts his finger on one of the names and says, "How about this one, old man?"

The old man says, "It doesn't matter which. No one's going to call me by that name anyway—or by any other name."

"Then, this will be recorded as your new name." The Korean detective tells the policeman the old man's "new" name—a Japanese name.

"All right," says the policeman. He writes the name in the ledger. "What about his family members?"

The Inspector comes back into the room, accompanied by another Japanese policeman. I know him. He is the Chief of Police.

My father exchanges bows with the Chief of Police.

The Chief of Police says, "Such inclement weather, and you honor us by being here in person. Is this your son?"

I edge nearer to my father.

The Chief of Police, a short man with bushy eyebrows and large eyes behind dark brown tortoise-shell glasses, looks at the Inspector and says, "Well, I trust the Inspector here will take care of your matter as speedily as he can. Anything, anytime I can be of any help or service, please call on me. I am, indeed, honored by your presence here in person."

My father and he exchange bows again. The Chief of Police goes out of the room, his black leather riding boots jangling and dragging his spurs on the wet floor.

My father takes out a piece of paper from his vest pocket. He hands it to the Inspector. "I assume," he says, "this is what you want, Inspector. I hope you will be pleased."

The Inspector looks at the paper. "Yes, yes," he says. "Iwamoto. . . . Ah—it is a very fine name, sir. It does justice to your person. It reminds me of your house by the mountain and, also, of your orchard, with all those rocky mountains around it. I will have it registered. You needn't wait for the certificate, needless to say. I will have someone bring it to your house later."

"Iwamoto" . . . "Iwamoto." I mouth the name. Our new name. My new name. "Iwa"—rock. "Moto"—root . . . base . . . foundation. "Rock-Foundation." So this is our "new" surname, our Japanese "family" name.

"Come," my father says to me.

The Korean detetctive leads us out, with the Inspector by my side. At the front door, which the detective holds open, the Inspector gives my father a salute. "I thank you, sir, for taking the trouble to come in person."

We step out into the cold. The snow is turning into a blizzard. The long line of people is still standing outside, hunched and huddled, rubbing their ears and faces, stamping their feet in the snow. My father pauses for a moment on the steps, one arm around my shoulders, and says:

"Look."

Afraid, bewildered, and cold, I look up at his face and see tears in his eyes.

"Take a good look at all of this," he whispers. "Remember it. Don't ever forget this day."

I look at all those people lined up, from the steps all the way to the gate and outside. I feel a tug at my hand, and I follow him down the steps. We walk by the people slowly, my father not speaking. They bow to him, some removing their hats. My father, bowing back, approaches the group of his friends still in line. In silence, they shake hands.

Then, we move on along the line of people standing in the snow. Some shake hands with my father; most of them merely bow, without words. We are outside the gate. There, too, a long line has formed and is still forming, all the way down the hill, past the gray stucco Methodist church . . . and I am thinking, "We lost our names; I lost my name; and these people are all going to lose their names, too, when they walk into the police station, into that half-empty large hall, when a 'new' name, a Japanese name, is entered in the big ledger with a pen dipped into a dark blue inkwell. . . ."

"What does our new name mean, sir?" I ask my father when we are down the hill and on the main street.

"Foundation of Rock," he says, shielding my face from the bitter-cold snow with his hand. ". . . on this rock I will build my church. . . ."

I do not understand him.

"It is from the Bible," he says.

*   *   *

By twelve o'clock, all the children in our class have new names. As soon as each class submits to the principal a complete list of all the new names, the class is sent out of the school to go to the Japanese shrine to pay its respects to the gods of the Empire and make its report to the Emperor—to announce that we now have Japanese names. At least once a week, each class is required to go to the shrine for an hour of meditation and prayer for the victory and prosperity of the Empire. It was our class's turn the day before, and we "prayed" for the victory and safety of the German *Luftwaffe* pilots who are bombing England in—as I shall learn years later to call it—the Battle of Britain.

Every town and every village now has a shrine—a miniature copy of the "main" shrine somewhere in Japan, where all the souls of the dead soldiers, for example, are supposed to go to rest. The shrine in our town is a small, wooden structure with a gable roof and several flights of stone steps built halfway up the mountain behind our house. The shrine is tended by a middle-aged Japanese Shinto priest, a bald-headed little man with a fat wife, who happens to live in a house that is next to ours, though carefully separated from ours by a bamboo fence.

The snow is coming down hard as we struggle up the narrow, icy path in file. Whenever there is a strong wind, the heavily laden pines shower down on us swarms of little icicles and snow. My bare hands are freezing, my bare ears are numb, and my feet are wet and cold with snow that slips inside my boots. Everyone's cheeks are red and raw from the icy wind. We gasp our way up the mountain. There is a small plaza at the foot of the stone steps, and the wind at the clearing is unbearable. The lashing, biting wind shrieks and whines all around us. The town below is invisible— lost in the blizzard, smothered by the raging snow. At the command of our teacher, I have to coax the children to gather and stand in formation. Then we kneel down in the snow, with our heads bowed. The teacher tells the priest, who has come down the steps from the shrine up above, that we are all there to report to the gods and the Emperor our new names. The priest, dressed in a purple-and-white priest's garment, wears a small sort of hat on his bald head. The teacher gives him the list of our new names. The priest reads the names one by one, slowly, bowing his head to the shrine above with each name. Then the priest chants something in a singsong voice, and, when he finishes the chanting, we all bow, now standing up. Snow clings to my pants, and my hands are wet from the snow. We look like a group of snow-men, covered as we are from top to bottom with the snow. At last we are dismissed by the priest, who goes back up the stone steps into the shrine, back to the sanctuary of his gods and the spirit of the Emperor that resides in it. Years later, when, at last, our Liberation comes, we raid the shrine, which is then already wrecked and has been set on fire by the townspeople, and, there, in the inner sanctuary, we discover a small wooden box; in it, we find, wrapped in rice paper, two wooden sticks to which we have been bowing and pray-ing all those years—the sticks from a tree on the "sacred" grounds of the "main" shrine in Japan. . . .

Our teacher dismisses the class for the day. The children, no longer in formation, scramble down the mountain path, without a word and without a sound. The teacher wants me to come with him. I follow him down the path in silence. I skid once on the way down and roll over, plunging into a deep pile of snow. He offers his hand and helps me up on my feet. His bare hand clasps my bare hand. He leads me down the mountain on the path, which forks at the foothill, one path going toward the school and the other going into the town, past our house. He takes the path that goes by our house. He is still holding my hand. I do not know how to disengage my hand from his. I do not want to be seen letting him hold my hand, but he grips it firmly and strides toward our house. We pass the Shinto priest's Japanese-style wooden house. We are at the east gate of our house.

Someone must have seen us coming down the path and told my father, because we find my father at the gate waiting for us. He has not changed his clothes.

My father and the teacher exchange bows.

I slip away from the teacher and stand by my father.

"No school this afternoon?" says my father to no one in particular.

I shake my head.

The teacher says, in Japanese, "Too much has happened to the children today already; so I sent them home for the day."

My father simply nods his head.

"I hope you don't mind my bringing him home," says my teacher, casting a quick glance at me.

"Not at all."

A moment of silence follows, all of us standing there in the pouring snow by the gate. I am wondering if my father will invite the teacher in, but he is quiet and shows no hint of asking the young Japanese in.

Then, the teacher gestures abruptly, as if to touch my face. "I am sorry," he says.

My father gives him a slight bow of his head.

"Even the British wouldn't have thought of doing this sort of primitive thing in India," says the Japanese.

I am at a loss, trying to comprehend what he says and means.

". . . inflicting on you this humiliation . . ." he is saying, ". . . unthinkable for one Asian people to another Asian people, especially we Asians who should have a greater respect for our ancestors. . . ."

"The whole world is going mad, sir," says my father quietly, "going back into another dark age. Japan is no exception."

My teacher nods. "As one Asian to another, sir, I am deeply ashamed."

"I am ashamed, too, sir," says my father, "perhaps for a reason different from yours."

My teacher, without a word, bows to my father, turns round, and disappears into the blinding snow.

"It is a small beginning," says my father, as he has said before about my Korean teacher, who is now somewhere in

Manchuria. He gives me a hug. "I am ashamed to look in
your eyes," he says—another one of those mysterious things
he likes to say. "Someday, your generation will have to forgive us." I don't know what he is talking about, but the
scene and the atmosphere of the moment, in the roaring
wind and with the snow gone berserk, make me feel dramatic.

"We will forgive you, Father," say I, magnanimously.

His arm tightens around my shoulders. "Come on," he
says, leading me into the house. "We have one more place to
go to. Your grandfather and I are going out to the cemetery.
Would you like to come?"

I nod. I am, suddenly, too overwhelmed and awed by
enigmas beyond my child's understanding to speak.

"I hope our ancestors will be as forgiving as you are," he
says. "It is a time of mourning."

And, only then, do I understand the meaning of the black
armband on his sleeve and on those of his friends.

                    *   *   *

About four miles out of town, between our house and the
orchard, the cemetery lies at the foot of a hill that gradually
rises up to become a craggy, rock-strewn, barren mountain.
It is what the townspeople call a common burying ground,
one that is used by poor people who cannot provide their
dead with a private cemetery—with the hope that, someday,
when they can afford a family burial plot, they will exhume
the dead and move them to their own, private graves. My
family is not poor—now; it was poor in the days of my great-
grandfather and of my grandfather, when he was young,
and, of course, before their time. All our known ancestors
are buried in the common burying ground, where I am now
plowing through the deep snow in the wailing wind—my
grandfather's parents and my grandmother's parents are
buried next to each other.

Twenty or thirty people are moving about the burying

ground. Some are in white; some, in gray, like my father
and my grandfather. All are shrouded with white snow; now,
some are kneeling before graves; some, brushing the snow
off gravestones; some, wandering about like lost souls. . . .

Halfway to the graves of our ancestors, we meet my father's
friend the doctor and his old mother, who are coming down
the hill. No one says a word, but the old woman silently
touches the sleeve of my grandfather's gray topcoat. Her gray
hair is undone and down in the fashion of women in mourning. Her hair is coated with snow and her eyebrows, too. She
is weeping, leaning on the arm of her son. We part in
silence.

Whenever we pass people on their knees before the graves
of their ancestors, we bow our heads. Some people are on
their way out of the grounds, and we move past each other
without words, just bowing to each other.

When we are in front of the graves of our ancestors, my
father wipes the snow off the gravestone. The names chiseled
on the gravestones are filled with ice, so that I can barely
distinguish the outlines of the letters.

The three of us are on our knees, and, after a long moment
of silence, my grandfather, his voice weak and choking with
a sob, says, "We are a disgrace to our family. We bring disgrace and humiliation to your name. How can you forgive
us!"

He and my father bow, lowering their faces, their tears
flowing now unchecked, their foreheads and snow-covered
hair touching the snow on the ground. I, too, let my face
fall and touch the snow, and I shiver for a moment with the
needling iciness of the snow on my forehead. And I, too, am
weeping, though I am vaguely aware that I am crying because the grown-ups are crying.

My grandfather unwraps a small bundle he brought with
him and takes out three wine cups and a bottle of rice wine.
He fills the cups with the wine, for all of us.

We hold the cups in our hands and pour the wine over

the graves, one by one, with my grandfather filling our cups with more wine before each mound. The pale liquid forms a small puddle for a second on the hard snow before it trickles down into the snow, as if someone inside the mound beneath the snow-packed earth is sipping it down.

Then, my grandfather fills our cups once more, and we hold them up high before our eyes for a moment and then drink.

My grandfather would like to be alone for a while. My father and I make a final bow to the graves and leave him.

More people are trudging in the snow, coming up to the burying ground. Here and there, I see people on their knees in front of graves, some crying aloud, some chanting, wailing mournful words. An old man in white—gasping in the freezing air and the blowing snow flurries, supported by a young woman, also in white and with her hair down and disheveled, stumbles in the knee-deep snow. He comes up to my father.

The old man stretches out his wrinkled, gnarled hand to my father, touching him. His long white beard is caked with snow. His small, bleary eyes, opaque and watery, peer out of the hollows formed by his high cheekbones.

His tremulous voice says to my father, "How can the world be so cruel to us? We are now ruined—all of us! Ruined!"

My father does not speak.

The young woman says, "Come on, Father, we must hurry home."

The old man says, "Now I lost my own name and I am as dead as . . ."

"Please!" the young woman begs.

And—suddenly—I am repelled by the pitiful sight of the driveling, groveling old man, whose whining muttering is lost in the bitter wind and swirling snow. Turning away from him, I stride down the path made by footsteps. I stop and turn around to see if my father is following me.

He is still with the old man, who is now clutching at the

arm of my father, openly wailing, and my father stands silently, with his head bowed. The young woman, too, standing behind the back of the old man, is weeping. Beyond them, I see my grandfather on his knees before the graves.

The snow keeps falling from a darkening sky, millions and millions of wild, savage pellets swirling and whishing about insolently before they assault us with malicious force. I watch the people everywhere, all those indistinct figures engulfed in the slashing snow, frozen still, like lifeless statuettes —and I am cold, hungry, and angry, suddenly seized with indescribable fury and frustration. I am dizzy with a sweet, tantalizing temptation to stamp my feet, scratch and tear at everything I can lay my hands on, and scream out to everyone in sight to stop—*Stop! Please stop!*—stop crying and weeping and sobbing and wailing and chanting. . . . Their pitifulness, their weakness, their self-lacerating lamentation for their ruin and their misfortune repulse me and infuriate me. What are we doing anyway—kneeling down and bowing our heads in front of all those graves? I am gripped by the same outrage and revolt I felt at the Japanese shrine, where, whipped by the biting snow and mocked by the howling wind, I stood, like an idiot, bowing my head to the gods and the spirit of the Japanese Emperor . . . and I remember my father's words: "I am ashamed to look in your eyes. Someday, your generation will have to forgive us." *Stop! Stop! Stop!* I want to shout out into the howling wind and the maddening snow. How long—for how many generations—are you going to say to each other, "I am ashamed to look in your eyes"? Is that going to be the only legacy we can hand down to the next generation and the next and the next?

"Oh, we are ruined!" Ha! What is the matter with you all, you grown-ups! All this whining, wailing, chanting, bowing to the graves, sorrowful silence, meaningful looks, burning tears . . . that is not going to save you from having to cry out, "Oh, ruination!" Damn, damn, damn—like my good old grandmother would say—Damn!

And—with the kind of cruelty only a child can inflict on adults—I scream out toward those frozen figures:

"I don't care about losing my name! I am just cold and *hungry!*"

And only then do I give in to a delicious sensation of self-abandonment—and I begin to cry.

My father is at my side. "We'll go home now."

With tear-filled eyes, I look up at him. "I am sorry, but . . ."

"Yes?"

"But—what good can all this do? What good will all this do for us?" I say defiantly, flinging my arms wide open to encompass the burying ground, with all its graves and the people; "What good will all this do to change what happened!"

To my surprise, he says quickly, "Nothing."

"Then, why do you? . . ."

"That's enough now," he says. "Someday, you will understand."

I am not soothed by these words, which are vague and hollow to a child's comprehension of the here and now. I do not respond to him.

He bends down, bringing his face close to mine. There is a strange smile on his face. "Today," he says, "you, too, have made a small beginning." Ah—Father—always a riddle.

"Come on," he says, extending his hand to help my grand-father onto the path. "Let us all go home now."

It is dark, and, with the coming of darkness and the night, the wind is dying down, and the snow is falling straight and calmly. The blurry figures of the people move about the burying ground like ghosts haunting the graves in the snow.

At the bottom of the hill, my father asks, "Would you like me to carry you on my back?"

I nod unabashedly and climb onto his back, nuzzling my frozen face against him, clinging to his broad shoulders.

And so, in such a way then, the three of us, the three generations of my family, bid farewell to our ancestors in their graves, which we can no longer see in the heavy snow, and join the others from the town to find our way back to our home.

Today, I lost my name. Today, we all lost our names.

February 11, 1940.

An Empire for Rubber Balls

At the first sign of dawn, my mother is up and in the kitchen and starts preparing the breakfast for the family. She must tend to five settings of breakfast these days. My father has his breakfast alone and has already gone out to the orchard by the time we, that is, I and my sister, are ready for ours. When we leave for school—my sister is in the second grade now—my mother gets the breakfast for our grandparents, and, when they are taken care of, she feeds my other sister, who is three, and my new baby brother. Then, at last, she and the two young maids sit down together and have their breakfast. My mother admits that it is a rather "hectic morning routine" but says that she is "fortunate enough to have the help of the two young girls." The young maid who had been with us since we came back from Manchuria is now married to a farmer and lives out of town. When she left, my mother at first said that she didn't need another maid, but, when the two teenage girls came to her with their mothers, who pleaded with her to "just feed them, clothe them, and give them a place to sleep," she gave in and agreed to take them in. The girls, skinny and in rags, didn't even want wages—afraid they might be turned away—though, of course, my mother insisted on paying them. They are from poor peasant families that are "starving to death," in the words of their mothers. Nowadays, many families in town have one or two maids, girls like our maids, not because they are well off and can afford to have maids but because taking these girls in is one way to help the peasant families. Our maids have never been to school—they can't read or write even Korean—so my mother is teaching them to read and write our own language, just as she is instructing my sister, the second-grader, because they are not teaching anything Korean at the school.

A war is going on in the Pacific between Japan and America and her allies. . . .

My sister and I finish our breakfast of millet, white-radish soup, and pickled vegetables, and we set off to school together.

My mother comes out to the east gate to see us off. "Are you staying after school today?" she asks me.

"Yes. We have to go through one more rehearsal." The school is presenting to the public a series of plays performed by the children. My class, the sixth grade, will have a play this evening—and I am in it. The occasion has something to do with the birthday celebration of the Imperial Crown Prince, who happens to be of my age. The play, a war drama written and directed by our teacher, a middle-aged Japanese, is about a platoon of Japanese soldiers in China taking time out to celebrate the Crown Prince's birthday, and so on. As the class leader, I have been made to play the part of a Japanese lieutenant, the platoon-leader, who, in the play, will deliver a long speech that is full of felicitations, pronouncements of loyalty to, and love for, the Imperial Family, and affirmations of the Empire's effort to conquer the whole of China and, now that Japan has been at war with America and England for over a year, to "destroy, annihilate, and break into smithereens all those barbaric, blue-eyed, hook-nosed Yankees and John Bulls." My father neither says a word about the play nor suggests a possible way out of my predicament. My mother says that, because I have had no choice as to what role I am to play, the townspeople will understand. . . . I have to wear a Japanese officer's uniform and saber—to say nothing of the speech I have to make. My grandmother says bluntly, "They are making you play the part because of your father." My grandfather simply frowns at the whole affair. I know there are other children in the class who would give anything to play the principal part in the play, that is, my part. But, our teacher is adamant and announces that he can't have "the leader of my class play the part of a private." A strange logic, because there are many in our class who speak Japanese better than I can and who are far better actors. My friends who are not in the play are needling me with cruel wisecracks such as "Just wait till your father sees you all dolled up in Japanese uniform with a saber and all!"

I tell my mother, once again, that I am ashamed of having to be in the play. "I could go to Pyongyang and stay with my grandparents, and you can tell the teacher I am sick or something."

She shakes her head. "That's telling a lie, isn't it? Well, just get it over with. No one is going to hold anything against you, simply because you were made to play this part."

I am aware that my mother is doing her best to soothe me and lighten my sense of predicament, but my uneasiness over the whole affair is weighing on my mind. I dare not tell her, for example, about what the Chinese man told me—the same Chinese man who is still running the same Chinese restaurant by the market place. The old Chinese man, who has always been friendly and partial to me, said to me, "What's the matter with you? Don't you know this is hurting your father's feelings?" That was when I and a friend of mine, who plays the part of a sergeant in the drama, and a few others went to his restaurant for fried noodles during a break in our rehearsal; I and the "sergeant" had sabers with us, the long sabers that were loaned to our teacher by the police; the Chinese man took one look at me as he emerged from his kitchen, beckoned me over to him, and told me off: "If you are going to come around to my place like that, you are not welcome here any more." I tried to explain to him the situation about the school play, and how I had no choice, and so on, but he merely shook his head: "Why you?" he said. Well, why me? I told him *that*, precisely, was the problem. Couldn't he understand? He simply puckered his mouth. "It is disgraceful," he muttered, disappearing back into the kitchen. Whether in anger with him or with myself, I told my friends to get out of the place, as I was not hungry and was going back to the school. I have not been back to the restaurant since. I feel like an outcast. . . .

I make one more try with my mother: "Isn't there any way Father can get me out of the play?"

My mother doesn't reply to my question.

"Come on," says my sister, tugging at my sleeve. "We are going to be late."

I do not move, waiting for my mother to say something, anything that will help me get through the day.

She looks at me for a moment and says, "I don't know what we can do about the play . . . but, before I forget again, let me go and get the money for you. Remember? We forgot about it." She goes back into the house.

My sister says again that we are going to be late.

I tell her to leave me alone—doesn't she understand that I have a problem?

She goes off by herself.

Just then, the young farmer comes out of the house, carrying a bucket filled with water. He puts the bucket down next to a pile of twenty or so bags of sand and a hoe and a mop. These things are there to "prepare ourselves against the enemy air raids," that is, just in case the American B-29 Superfortress that flies over us regularly, once a week, a tiny, silvery speck high up in the sky, may decide to drop bombs on us. We have to keep the buckets full of water at all times, because the water evaporates quickly, just sitting out in the hot sun; also, we have to keep the sand in the paper bags dry by covering the bags with straw mats when it rains.

At the west gate—outside of it, to be exact—we have an identical setup. Every house must have them by the gate or by the door, where everyone can see them. Once a week, there is a fire drill at the market place. In addition to the sand, water, hoe, and mop, every house-owner must construct an underground air-raid shelter. Because we have an underground storage place for our apples, my father thought that would do, but the police insisted that we had to make one, in any case. My father and the young farmer dug a large hole by the storage place, covered it with timber and straw mats, and put wooden boards on the ground inside the hole. It is big enough for six or seven of my friends to play in it, a dank, dark place that smells of dirt and wet straw mats. During each fire drill, the whole family must be inside the shelter, except for my father and the young farmer, who would, together, have to put the fire out if American bombs ever fell.

We know, however, that the American bombers would never drop a single bomb on us in Korea, because, once, a B-29 Superfortress dropped thousands of leaflets, which said that, because the Korean people were not their enemies, the Americans would not bomb Korean towns and villages. The promise was signed by General Douglas MacArthur, the Supreme Commander of American Forces in the Pacific, and by Dr. Syngman Rhee, the chairman of the Provisional Government of Korea in Exile. Although the leaflets didn't find their way down to our house, they fell from the blue sky like big snowflakes all over the town and the mountains and the hills behind our house. The Japanese Police went around for several days, checking every house, to collect and confiscate the leaflets. The school children were mobilized, too, and were swarming over the hills behind the school, collecting the leaflets. The message in the leaflets was in Korean, so most of the children weren't able to understand it, except for those in the fifth grade and beyond who could remember Korean. As the class leader, I had to collect all the leaflets our class picked up and hand them over to the principal; I pocketed one, since I understood the message in Korean, and brought it to my father. He warned me not to tell anyone we had an American leaflet in our house.

In fact, however, I was less intrigued by the content of the leaflets than by the thought that they had come to us all the way across the ocean from America; I imagined bundles and bundles of leaflets being loaded onto an American bomber, which would take off from a secret air base somewhere in the Pacific, probably in Australia or in China, and fly over us. In my imagination, I could hear the voices of the American airmen, and possibly a Korean patriot aboard, too, as they were getting ready to drop the leaflets—the Americans saying, "Here they go!" and the Korean patriot shouting in joy, "Look! Look! That town below is my hometown!" or something to that effect.

All during the Pacific war, which the Japanese called the "Greater Asian War," we in Korea were never once bombed; as far as I remember, there was only one incident in which something other than leaflets was dropped by an American plane; this occurred when a plane jettisoned a reserve fuel tank, which fell into a rice paddy somewhere in the vicinity of Seoul; the Japanese would have us believe that it was a bomb, and they made a film of it. My father, who saw the newsreel with me, said, "I'd always thought a bomb that is to be dropped from a high altitude had to have fins." The bomb-shaped fuel tank didn't have any fins. My father knows something about bombs, I suspect, although not too much about aerial bombs. . . .

A puzzling thing about the sand, the bucket of water, the hoe, the wet mop, and the rest is, as my mother says, that they have to be placed by the gate outside each house. My father says the police have to be able to see them from outside to see if everyone is obeying their instructions. They inspect our "preparedness" once a week. The young farmer says that, if there was a fire inside the house, by the time he ran to the gates to get the sand and water and so on, the house would have burned down. He laughs and laughs, saying to my parents, "What will they come up with next?" He will find out soon enough, when he has to sharpen several dozen bamboo sticks that we have to contribute to the police armory, keeping three in the house, as instructed by the police—one for my father, one for me, and one for himself. The sharpened sticks are for use in case the Americans land on Korea—we are expected to charge against the Americans on the beach and bamboo them to death. . . .

Speaking of the bamboo sticks: The upper-class children at the school must go through a weekly drill with bamboo spears, sticking them into straw dummies (on stakes) that represent American soldiers; the drill is supervised by an old Japanese lieutenant in the reserve, one of the military instructors now assigned to all schools, including grade schools. The fifty-two-year-old lieutenant is very good with his sword, and, frequently, he will charge the straw dummies and cut them in half, swinging his gleaming sword left and right, screaming out—in Japanese, of course—"Sons of American bitches!" It is a fascinating virtuoso performance that dazzles the children, who have to make more new straw dummies to be tied onto new wooden stakes, a process that takes a few days because we have to go around collecting straw, ropes, and stakes from farmers, and so we don't have the drill for the time being. . . .

My mother comes back out to the gate and gives me five coins. Nowadays, all of us come to school always with some coins, just in case we are caught speaking Korean. Whenever we are found speaking Korean or whenever any teacher thinks we are speaking Korean, we get punished, first with five strokes of the cane on our legs and then with a fine—a coin, which we drop into a tin can. The can is sealed at the top and has a slit for the coins, and it is placed directly under a big chart that has our names; each time we drop a coin into the tin can, we have to mark an "X" in a column by our name. When the tin can is filled with our coins, usually once a week, I have to take it to the principal, who will count the coins and record the amount. On the following Monday, the principal will declare, at our morning assembly, that such and such class has contributed the most money during the preceding week toward building Japanese Kamikaze planes, tanks, or guns, depending on where the money is supposed to be going that week, and the "winning" class—the class that put the most money in its tin can—will receive a prize such as a new mop or a new bucket; so, when our class needs a new mop or a new bucket . . . When my father hears about it, he says to my mother, "It is Kafkaesque." Kafka, he tells me, was an Austrian writer who wrote strange stories about all sorts of strange things people do to each other. . . .

"I'll tell you what," says my mother, interrupting my thought. "How long is that speech in the play?"

"Quite long. It takes me almost ten minutes to say it all."

She smiles. "Well, can you remember it, the whole speech, word by word?"

"Of course, I can."

"Suppose you can't. I mean, suppose you just couldn't recite the speech from memory."

"You mean—while the play is on?"

She nods. "It is a long, long speech, after all. Not many children can be expected to recite a speech that long by heart."

"I may get stuck in the middle of it."

"That could happen, don't you think?"

"It sure is a long speech."

"I know."

"I may get too nervous, with all those people in the audience."

"That could happen, too."

I am trying my best to suppress the ecstasy and the urge to explode into laughter that is pumping inside me. I look solemn and worried. "Well, if I get too nervous on the stage and can't recite the speech all the way through, wouldn't the people think I am pretty dumb?"

"Some people may. Your teacher would probably think so."

"He wouldn't put me in another play, then."

"I suppose not."

"What would Father think?"

"I am sure he won't say you are a dumb boy."

I pretend I am mulling it over. "Well, I won't tell Father, if you won't."

"I don't know what there is to tell him about," she says. "Come to think of it, what made me ever think you may not be able to recite the speech by heart? I wonder who gave me that silly idea?"

"Father?"

She tilts her face. "I don't know. I don't think so, do you?"

"I think he did."

"Whatever you think. Now, go on to school. I am sure your play will be a big success. We'll all be there tonight."

"Grandmother? Did Grandmother? . . ."

"Never mind about that. Go on now."

I am laughing so hard that I can't speak. Good old Grandmother!

"She has a brain," says my mother, laughing, too.

I wave to her and run off from the house.

*   *   *

There is no school in the morning, as happens often these days. Whenever we have a lecture by a visiting military officer or a showing of a war film or when the American B-29 Superfortress appears in the sky, classes are suspended. This morning, at the morning assembly, we are told to go home first and then go around the town, stopping by every house in our assigned areas to collect all the rubber balls we can find.

My class is responsible for the sector that our house is in. I have to divide the class into five groups to cover the whole sector. Our teacher says that those who come back with the most rubber balls will get a prize.

The rubber balls . . . When the Japanese troops occupied Singapore and all of Malaya and Borneo, the world's greatest rubber-producers, all children in the Empire, including Korean children, were given a rubber ball to celebrate the capture of these vital rubber-producing areas from the British and other enemies of the Empire. The rubber balls bore stamped letters that said, "Ten Thousand Years for the Occupation of Singapore and Malaya." I got a big white ball, one of the few big balls awarded to our class; most of the other children got small balls, the size of a tennis ball. Between myself and my sister, we have three rubber balls, because she, the class leader of her class, simply kept an extra ball, a left-over, for herself. That was only several months ago, a month or so before the naval Battle of Midway. . . . Since then, there was the naval Battle of the Solomons, and the American Marines have landed in Guadalcanal. In Europe, the Germans, their Mutual Nonaggression Treaty with the Russians torn up long ago, are laying siege to Stalingrad. . . .

. . . the rubber balls . . . The Japanese want the rubber balls back. That's what I tell my mother, who is surprised to see me home so soon. I am with three of my friends, each of us carrying a sackful of rubber balls of all sizes.

"Rubber balls?" says my mother. "They want them back? Why?"

I shrug my shoulders.

"Well!" She peeks into our sacks. "They must need rubber very badly."

I collect three rubber balls from the house. My sack is full, and my big ball wouldn't fit in. I dump out all the balls from the sack, thinking that, perhaps, the big ball should go in first. The balls roll out and bounce around the courtyard. My friends chase after them, shrieking with laughter, making themselves look silly, ending up throwing their sacks of balls into the air. Balls and balls—white, pink, blue, yellow balls are bouncing around all over. We are kicking them, stepping on them, throwing them at each other, shouting and running around.

My grandmother comes out of the kitchen. "What is going on?"

My mother tells her about the occasion.

"I need a bigger sack to put all of them in," I say to my mother.

My grandmother says, "Why waste another sack? Let the air out."

"What?"

"Let the air out," she says. "Make a couple of holes in each ball and you can squash them in."

One of my friends says, "Why didn't we think of that before?"

Soon, we have all the balls punctured with nails and deflated and squeezed into flat, saucer-like shapes, and stacked up. We put them in our sacks and start back to the school.

Back at the school, all the classes except the girls are assembled in the field. In front of the formation of each class, each class leader must pile up all the rubber balls his class has collected. Cardboard boxes, sacks made of straw or cloth, and a few wooden crates full of balls—big, small, soft, or hard balls of all sizes and colors. My class has only one big sack of balls; I have had my classmates puncture all the balls they have collected, and I have had all the deflated balls stuffed into one large sack. A lone sack of balls, then, stands beside me in front of my class.

The Teacher of the Day, accompanied by the Student of the Day, checks each class. The Japanese teacher of athletics gets the report from each class leader, who tells him how many rubber balls his class has brought back. The teacher records the figure in his notebook; then, the class leader and the Student of the Day count the balls. When the figure is verified, the class is dismissed from the field.

For some reason, the athletics teacher walks past my class and continues his inspection, dismissing classes one by one. At last, all the classes are gone from the field, except mine. The Student of the Day, the class leader of another sixth-grade class, who is a friend of mine, gives me a shrug of his shoulders, with a worried look on his face. The athletics teacher, without turning to us, is going away toward the teachers' building.

"Sir?" says the Student of the Day, going after him, "You forgot . . ."

The teacher turns around. "Ah—you are still there," he says. "I forgot you were still there." He comes over to our class.

I am trying hard to control myself; I feel my body shaking. I report to him that my class has collected one hundred and twenty-three rubber balls, all in the sack.

He doesn't believe my figure. "Where are all the balls?"

I point my finger to the sack at my feet. "All in there, sir." I help the Student of the Day take out the squashed and neatly stacked balls and count them. I am squatting down, lining the balls up by their sizes, in rows of twenty each. I stand up, saying, "One hundred twenty . . ."

The teacher's fist punches me in the cheek.

I am knocked off my feet. I am sprawled on the dirt.

"Get up!"

I struggle up and, swaying, try to stand at attention. I taste dirt in my mouth and on my lips. My black uniform is covered with the reddish brown dirt. The Student of the Day picks up my cap and hands it to me. I slap the cap against my leg, once, twice, slowly, thinking—I must be calm, I must be calm, I must not be afraid. . . . Through the mist in my eyes, I vaguely see the dust flying from the cap and from my uniform. I put the cap on.

The teacher slaps me on the left cheek.

I wince, but I do not cry out. I taste blood in my mouth. I lick my lips. I rub my cheeks. Then—telling myself, "Speak loudly, speak calmly so that everyone can hear"—I ask the teacher, "Why did you hit me, sir?"

He kicks at the pile of our rubber balls.

The balls—pieces of rubber squashed and squeezed together like suction cups—are all over, in front of my class.

I turn around and face my class. "Go and pick up the balls." No one moves. "I said, 'Pick up the balls.' " Two of my friends come forward.

"Stay where you are!" says the teacher.

"Sir!" I say. "We have to rehearse the play for this evening, so I would like to have our class excused, sir."

He looks at me in silence.

"Why did you hit me, sir?" I ask him again. "I don't know what wrong I have done, sir. We collected more balls than lots of other classes did. I am going to report to my teacher that you hit me, sir."

"Why did you have all the balls punctured?"

"Sir?"

"Why did you ruin all the balls!"

"I couldn't fit all of them in the sack, sir." Suddenly, I know I am going to be stubborn, almost perversely so. The sensation is rather delicious, though I sense a slight tremor passing through my body. I feel myself relax and calm down. "Besides, sir," I say, "it was rubber, really, that we were to collect, not the balls, as you surely understand, sir."

I think I sense all the children in my class stiffen with

fear behind me, though they are also infected with a sense of thrill.

"Who told you that?" he says.

"No one, sir, but it was obvious, don't you think, sir?"

"Who told you that!"

"It is like the time we confiscated gold, silver, and even brass, isn't it, sir? Gold rings, gold bracelets, silver pins, and things like that, remember, sir? We were told then that these precious metals were needed to win the war. So I knew rubber is now needed to win the war, not the rubber balls, sir. Am I wrong, sir?"

He raises his fist, as if to strike me again, but he doesn't.

I go on, half being carried away and half knowing that there is now no turning back. "It never occurred to me that we were to collect rubber balls as such, sir, for other children to play with them, for example, sir. Like Japanese children on the mainland, sir. But then, sir, I wouldn't think Japanese children would want to play with the rubber balls we have played with, would you, sir?"

"The class is dismissed!" he shouts. "You, come with me!"

"Yes, sir."

He orders the Student of the Day to collect the "balls" and bring them to the principal's office.

My classmates are immobile and silent.

"I said, 'You are dismissed'!" says the teacher, with his hands on his hips. "Go!"

No one stirs; no one speaks. Everyone is looking down at the ground. We are the only children on the field. I can see the girls in their classrooms by the field, looking out toward us, their faces pressed against the windows.

"Class dismissed!"

My classmates stand still, bowing their heads.

I am triumphant. I tell the class, "You can all go back to the room and wait for me."

They look up at me.

One of them says, "We'll wait for you here."

Tears come to my eyes. I feel big and strong. "Go and have your lunch, and, if I don't come back soon, you can come out here and wait for me."

Some nod their heads.

I call the name of one of my friends. "You take charge while I am gone."

They begin to stir, and some shuffle away, kicking at the dust.

"Stay where you are!" says the teacher. "You will all stand out here until I come back!"

I am in a rage—and I say to my classmates, in Korean, "Why didn't you go when I told you to? I'll be all right with this bastard. Anyway, thanks!"

The teacher's big hand grabs the back of my neck. "That's the end of you!" he shouts, dragging me away. "You treacherous beast!"

I am shoved through the door of the teachers' room, where each teacher has a desk in a cubbyhole. It is lunch time, and some twenty teachers—Japanese and Korean, men and women —are having their lunch. They all look up when I am flung into the room. No one says a word. I do not see my teacher. The Japanese athletics teacher is nearly holding me up in the air, hooking his fingers into the back of my collar, choking me. A Japanese, who was the teacher of our class in the fourth grade, the skinny "poet"—Chopstick—gets up from the ring of teachers who are sitting on chairs, around a big table in the middle of the room, eating lunch.

"What happened?" he says.

"This brat's head is crammed with dangerous thoughts," says the athletics teacher, pushing me forward.

Chopstick asks me, "What did you do?"

I do not answer. They are all alike, I think. Asking me what I did. What did *I* do? . . . Doesn't it ever occur to him to ask the teacher what *he* did? The big clenched fist drills into my back, propelling me forward. The athletics teacher is

picking out a bamboo sword, which is used for fencing practice, from a rack by the door to the principal's office.

The door opens from within, and the old Army lieutenant
comes out, the spurs jingling on his shiny brown riding
boots.

"What did he do this time?" the lieutenant says.

"Bad, bad!"

I see through the open door into the principal's office.

A policeman in black uniform is exchanging bows with the
principal. I see the bald head of the principal bow twice.

The policeman is saluting the principal.

We are standing by the door.

The Student of the Day comes over to us with the sack of
the "balls" my class has collected. He stands by us, holding
onto the sack, not knowing what to do with it.

The policeman comes out of the room, with the old
principal a step behind him. The round, wrinkled face of the
principal peers out from behind the policeman.

"That brat again?" says the principal.

The policeman, an Inspector, a tall, slim man, holding
his saber with his left hand, looks at me. He must be new
in town, I think, because I have not seen him before.

The principal tells the policeman who I am, the son
of —.

The Inspector nods.

The athletics teacher tells the principal what happened on
the field—about the rubber balls, and so on. I am said to
have insulted the teacher, disobeyed him, and, above all,
spoken dangerous thoughts in front of the class; I deserve to
be punished. And the teacher abruptly reaches for the sack
bulging with the "balls" and yanks it from the hand of the
Student of the Day, who, in confusion and apprehension,
lets go of the sack before the teacher's hand grabs it—and
the sack drops onto the floor, spilling the "balls" all over.

The athletics teacher slaps the Student of the Day on the
cheek, yelling, "Pick them up and get out!"

The principal gives the policeman a quick, slight bow, and goes back into his room.

The old Japanese lieutenant creaks by me. I hear him walking toward the group of teachers having their lunch, shouting to a Korean girl who is passing around cups of tea to the teachers, "Bring me a cup of tea!"

The Inspector is still standing there by the closed door.

The teacher drags me by the neck and pushes me toward the wall by the principal's door.

Outside the teachers' room, in the hallway, two boys are standing against the wall, each holding up a chair above his head. I have stood like that often, all day sometimes, for this or that offense; my arms would grow numb with pain and sag at the elbows; a teacher would come and slash at my arms with a thin strip of bamboo. . . .

I know the routine. I unbuckle my belt and let my pants fall and bunch down at my feet. I bend over, with my hands pressed against the wall.

"Apologize!" says the teacher.

I do not speak.

"If you apologize to me, you will get only ten strokes and I will let you go this time."

I know I am not going to speak.

I hear the swish-swish of the bamboo sword behind me as he cuts the air with it.

A voice says, "Perhaps, I can talk to the boy."

Out of the corner of my eye, I see the Inspector looking at the teacher.

"This is *our* problem," says the teacher. "Not *yours*."

I sense an edge in the teacher's voice, and I know that he spoke loudly so that all in the room could hear.

The Inspector says, "I know the boy's father. Well, you know who he is. I would like to remind you that one reason I have been assigned to this town by the governor of the province concerns the boy's father, if you understand what I mean." Then, without waiting for the reply, he says to me—in Korean—"If you apologize to him, I will see to it that you will be spared."

"Don't speak Korean! How dare you!" shouts the athletics teacher to the Inspector.

"Shut up!" says the Inspector, in Japanese, very loudly. "Perhaps, you do not realize that I am an officer of the Higher Police!"

The teacher is silent.

The Inspector says, "Do you know what that means?"

I know what the Higher Police means: a bureau of Japanese Police that controls Intelligence, the Thought Police, and —many suspect—the Secret Police.

The Inspector turns to me. "Now," he says.

I turn my face away toward the field. I can see my classmates standing in formation.

The Inspector says in Korean, "I am a Korean. Do you know that? I am a good friend of your father's. So, will you listen to me?"

I do not believe a word of it.

A moment of silence—and he says, still in Korean, "I am also a good friend of your uncle's, your uncle in the Manchurian Army. We went to school together."

I am looking at the cracks in the wall.

"You are as stubborn as your father—all of you," says the Inspector. "Don't you believe that I am your father's friend and your uncle's as well?"

I shake my head. "I believe you are an officer of the Higher Police."

And, suddenly—with a whish—the bamboo sword smashes my bottom, jolting me with a numbing blow that instantly shoots thousands of sharp needles of pain through my body, snapping it into an arch, flinging my head backward. My body is shaking, and my knees trembling, and I can't control my body. I press my lips tight and close my eyes with all my strength, but I can't shut the tears in. I taste the salty tears on my lips, but I make no sound. The bamboo sword is slashing into my flesh, onto my legs, my bottom, my back, each blow contorting my body and blinding me for a second. Then—suddenly—my tears stop and my body goes limp, and I think I hear a voice saying, "That's enough!" but the bamboo sword keeps smashing my body—yet, I am calm, so calm that I am almost surprised, as if I slipped out of my body so that I won't feel the pain. I can take it, I can take it, I think, feeling strangely serene and almost powerful; every fiber of my being is alive and pulsating with a sense of triumph, not hatred, of pride, not heroic bravery, and of being larger than life. Don't cry. . . . They know not what they do. . . . Love and Compassion for sinners and evildoers. . . . Turn the other cheek, also. . . . Be noble in suffering. . . .

But that self-induced, masochistic euphoria—an illusion—does not last long. There is no nobility in pain; there is only degradation. And, now, every sensation within me is turning, with each blow, into a boundless contempt, and my contempt is burning into hatred, a hatred fierce and immense—until, screaming, I am bending down, pulling up my pants, and the bamboo sword is striking me everywhere, on my back, my neck, my head—and I am crouching down, buckling my belt, and, now standing up, screaming and screaming, blinded by my hatred and rage, I lunge at the man, my head smashing into his underbelly, my fists punching into his groin. The man drops his bamboo sword, clutches at the back of my jacket, and flings me down onto the floor. I land on my side and see the man double up for a second, and then, after straightening up, he charges at me. I struggle up almost collapsing and in that split second I see the Inspector swiftly pick up the bamboo sword and strike the Japanese man on the back, hard, so hard that the bamboo sword, as if stuck to the man's back, follows him as he is knocked off his feet and is tumbling down to the floor by my feet, and I collapse, too, and, still screaming, I faint. . . .

*   *   *

There is a blank in my memory—but my mother is saying, "A boy being carried home, bleeding and swollen, and unconscious. No, you don't forget *that*."

No, you don't forget *that*. No, I won't forget *that*. I exult in neither bitterness nor hatred nor an ephemeral snobbishness of suffering; yet, I glory in neither magnanimity nor understanding nor forgiveness. I merely reflect, with a quick, sharp ache within me, that *that* is only one of the many other things that I cannot and will not forget. "Vengeance is Mine," says a god. "Vengeance is Yours," I say, "Memories are Mine."

". . . and the Inspector was so tense, so frightened," my mother is saying. "He kept on insisting that we had to get your father; he had to see your father right away. Your father was out at the orchard, meeting someone from China, and it was a secret meeting, and I had to keep the Inspector away from him. You were supposed to have said something terrib'e, something dangerous, and the Inspector was afraid that any one of the Korean teachers in the room could tell the Japanese what you were screaming about in Korean. Remember?"

"I am not sure."

"At first, I wouldn't believe it," she says, "thinking perhaps the Inspector was trying to play some sort of trick. You wouldn't be foolish enough to say a thing like that in front of all the teachers, but I guess you lost control. 'My father says Japan will lose the war in two years and when that day comes I will come back and kill you all.' No wonder the Inspector was so tense. Remember?"

I shake my head. "No."

"When he told me what you said before you fainted," she goes on, "I was frightened, too. He insisted he had to see your father to warn him, just in case, you know. He would keep an eye on the Thought Police people to see if any Korean teacher would come to them with information, and he also wanted us to send a telegram to your uncle in Manchuria to come home as soon as he could. The Inspector

thought that your uncle—he was a captain then, wasn't he?—
well, he thought your uncle's presence might be useful.
Something about having a mitigating influence on the
police. . . ."

The Manchurian Army, by then, was practically incor-
porated into the Japanese Kanto Army in Manchuria, which
was very powerful politically, and my uncle was a captain
in the Manchurian Army. My uncle . . . my idol, powerful, big, and generous. Only my father knew that he was
clandestinely in touch with the Koreans fighting for the
Chinese Army against the Japanese. Later, when the defeat
of Japan seemed imminent, my father sent him a message
to disappear and go underground. Too late. He was captured by the Soviet troops, who either could not care less
who he really was or already knew—he was working with the
wrong group of Koreans in exile, the non-Communist fac-
tion; the Soviets shot him, along with Japanese officers. . . .

"Uncle came home right away, didn't he?" I say.

My mother nods. "When your father came home from the
orchard, he met the Inspector and told him, yes, Japan
will indeed lose the war in two years; so he'd better start
thinking about himself. The Inspector became quite helpful
and useful after that. He asked your father what he could do.
At least, he was always honest with your father. He was a
classmate of your uncle's in Manchuria. When they were
children, his family once lived next door to your father's
family, and he always called your father his big brother. Anyway, your father told him he could start being helpful to the
leaders of the Korean community in town and keep an eye
on the Japanese police. Your father knew that there was a
contingency plan for the police, and he knew that, when the
Japanese knew they were defeated, they would round up the
Koreans on their black list and shoot them. Well, the
Inspector would keep an eye on that, among other things. He
also supplied your father and his friends with a list of
Korean informers for the police. In return, they promised

him they would give him safe-conduct and vouch for him after the liberation.

"So, you see, there he was, the Inspector, coming and going, and, then, your Japanese teacher came to the house, all excited and apologetic and not knowing what to do with the play your class was supposed to present that evening. 'I need your son for the play,' he kept on saying, and I said, 'Take a look at the boy and see for yourself if he is in any condition to appear in the play.' He didn't know what to do."

The teacher had to think fast, and he asked my friend who was to play the sergeant to take over my role. "But I can't recite the speech by heart, sir," said my friend. "Don't worry," said the teacher. "I will be directly in front of the stage with the speech written out on large sheets of paper. You can read it. There is no time, and there is no other way." But, at the last minute, the plans for the evening were changed, and the event would be held in the Presbyterian church rather than in the school auditorium, as originally planned. The stage in the small auditorium was a low platform, and the teacher could sit in the front row holding up the speech for my friend to see. But the platform in the church was higher than where the audience sat in the pews. The teacher would have to stand up right at the foot of the platform with the speech, and everyone in the audience would be able to see what was going on. Someone—the principal, the police, who knows?—changed the plans and decided that the Presbyterian church was the best place to stage a war drama performed by the school children in Japanese military uniform and wearing rifles and swords. . . .

". . . and, then, all of your class descended on the house, and they all wanted to see you," says my mother. "You were in bed, and you could hardly get up, let alone walk, and the doctor was coming, and your grandmother wanted to treat all your friends! Then, some of the Korean teachers came, and that Japanese teacher you had in the fourth grade—remember—he, too, came, not saying a word, just bowing to me and to your grandmother. Good thing your grandfather was out of town that day. He would have had a fit, and who knows what he might have done? And the neighbors started coming, all our relatives, and, for a while, it looked as if the whole town were coming to the house. You were bandaged so much you could barely stand up." She laughs and says, "I still don't know how you sneaked out of the house and made it to the church that evening. Plain stubbornness and, I must say, a dash of perversity, too."

A dash of perversity . . . Yes. I laugh. "That's right. But I made it, though. It took me a long time. I had to take one step at a time, sort of sideways." I can remember now. . . .

. . . someone in the dark, a woman in our neighborhood, finds me waddling down the street and says, Where do you think you are going like that, in the dark, in that shape? She knows what happened to me that noon. I am taking you back to your house, she says. I keep going, not responding to her. Are you out of your mind? she says. You will fall down and break your skull. Where are you going anyway? I am going to the church. To church? Why? I don't answer. Oh, I see, she says. But she doesn't know that the school children are performing in plays at the church. I'll help you to the church, she says. No, please, leave me alone. I can go myself. Oh, all right, but I am going to tell your parents, she says. Do they know you are out? Well, they ought to know where you are. I'll bet they are looking for you. I don't bother to reply one way or the other. I move on.

The bandages are rubbing against the open wounds on my bottom and legs and back, and, with each step I take, I wince, nearly crying out once. I am inching up the hill to where the church is, on the narrow dirt path, pressing my hands against the bandages to keep them from bunching up. Bandages are all over my body. Suddenly, I hear the voice of our young tenant farmer, calling my name in the dark. I keep quiet. I hear his footsteps coming up the path, and, then, he is by my side. I am not going back to the house, I say. I am not taking you home; I am going to carry you on my back to the church. He squats down, and I lean against his back. He grabs my ankles and, as I put my arms around his neck, he lifts me up. You are a sight to behold, he says. Did my father send you? Yes. Did he say for you to carry me to the church? Yes. I think about it for a moment. That's my father, you know, I say. Yes, he says, you are both alike. I am proud of him, I say. He is proud of you, too, he says; I know that for sure. The sky is clear, and the stars are out; the night air is pale and not so dark, but, around the church, it is black because of the lights inside the church. I direct him to take me around the church building to the back entrance. I want to go into the room where the church choir members keep their gowns and hymn books and assemble before they go out to the platform to take their seats by the altar. I ask him to let me down by the door, and I tell him to go in and look for my friend who is to play the part of the lieutenant—my part. My friend and a few others sneak out. Our class's turn will come in ten minutes or so. I hush them and tell them that I am going to be in the play. Don't tell the teacher about my being here, I say. Let's get in, and I will hide. . . .

". . . you didn't know that your father and I were right behind you, did you?" says my mother.

"No. It didn't occur to me to ask the farmer. But you didn't know what I was up to, did you?"

"Not for a while, but, when we saw you going in the back entrance, I guess we knew what you were going to do."

"And you let me go through with it."

"Why not? We knew what you would do. I told your father. Remember? What we had said about the speech in the play that morning?"

"Yes."

"So we slipped in through the front door while you were
sneaking in through the back door." She laughs. "Like
fugitives, and in our own church, too."

. . . all my friends in the play collaborate with me, hushed,
though exulting, in the bondage of our conspiracy. I am
hiding in the closet where the choir members' gowns are
stored, waiting for an all-clear knock. My teacher is bustling
around, rasping out instructions, reminders, and warnings.
It is now time for our class's play—and I am still in the closet.
We have arranged that my friend who was to be the sergeant
in the play but is playing the lieutenant would go through
the play until the moment comes for him to deliver the
speech. Fortunately, the script calls for him to emerge
from his "headquarters"—from off stage, that is—to appear
in front of the "soldiers" assembled for the occasion of His
Imperial Highness the Crown Prince's birthday. My friend
will knock on the closet door, and I will put on his uniform
and the saber while the "soldiers" on the stage "reminisce"
about their homes and families. Then, I will march onto—
hobble onto—the stage. . . .

". . . it was a sight," says my mother. "So—there you were,
dragging yourself out onto the stage, leaning on that long
saber as if it were a cane, your face puffed up and bruised,
and you could hardly walk straight. And, of course, everyone
knew what happened to you at the school. You could hear
the gasps and whispering going on in the audience. Then, it
was absolutely silent. And—nothing happened."

"I did say a few words, though."

"Oh, yes," she says, her voice laughing. "Ladies and gentlemen, today is supposed to be the birthday of the Imperial
Crown Prince, who happens to be of my age. In Korean,
too. Imagine!"

. . . but I quickly switch to Japanese, as if I just remem-
bered that I was supposed to be a Japanese officer. "Ladies
and gentlemen, . . ." Heaven knows why the teacher wrote

that into the script. . . . "Ladies and gentlemen, . . ." There I am, on the stage, facing the audience, ignoring the teacher (who is at the foot of the stage, frantically waving the sheets of paper in his hand), ignoring the front rows where all the teachers sit, and saying now in Japanese, ". . . today is the glorious birthday of our Crown Prince, and I would like to say a few words to you from the bottom of my heart, as we are gathered here together, we the Imperial soldiers, in the desolate plains of China . . ." And that is the end of my speech, because I am not saying anything more. I am standing there, leaning on the long saber, looking at the quiet audience, becoming oblivious of the time's passage, of the gradual commotion building up in the audience, of the principal and the teachers, now whispering to one another, and of my teacher, calling my name in a frenzied whisper, hissing—"Go on! Go on!"

". . . and you just stood there, not saying a word, and looking as if you were going to collapse any moment," my mother says, "and, I must say, looking rather grotesque, with your bruised, swollen face daubed with ointment and mercurochrome. . . ."

And what was on my mind then? What went through my mind? What was my "grotesque" face showing? What silent words were my cut, bloated lips forming? What were my open wounds hidden beneath the blood-soaked bandages trying to say?

". . . then, all of a sudden, tears were running down your cheeks, though you weren't making any sound," my mother says quietly. Tears glisten in her eyes—two decades later. "And you just walked off the stage, and all your classmates were following you out. . . ."

. . . but I am thinking . . ."All of a sudden, tears were running down your cheeks. . . ." What was on my mind while I stood, speechless, on that stage? What words would my bloodied lips have said if they could? And why the tears?

Why—why was I weeping? For me?—for my parents?—for my people down there?—for my friends? Or—for everyone, Koreans and Japanese alike? For the conquerors and the conquered alike? Why the tears? I do not know.

"Perhaps for wounded souls," says my mother. "Everywhere."

"Is Someone Dying?"

Yesterday, those who did not have blisters on their hands were given a pick and a shovel and were ordered to work on the runway. Along with my classmates, I shoveled all day, digging up rubbery red clay, to a depth of four feet, barely clearing a ten- by twenty-foot sector, which was our class's quota for the day. We are building an airfield about thirty miles south of Pyongyang—or about twenty miles north of our town. The airfield, we are told, will have two runways they are running out of pilots so fast, they can't keep planes that are being flown from Manchuria to the mainland. That the planes are to come all the way from Manchuria means— a friend of mine says, with a knowledgeable air—that either the Japanese are running out of planes in Japan proper or they are running out of pilots so fast, they can't keep planes flying in Manchuria.

In any case, so far, we have been spending most of our second year in junior high school in Pyongyang, on this so-called airfield, so-called because, although some four hundred to five hundred high school students have been working on it at all times for the last several months, the airfield has only one runway barely completed, and we have yet to see a single Kamikaze plane, or any plane, either land on the field or even fly over it.

We all live in tents, one class to a tent; after several months in use, the tents still exude a rancid odor of tar and grease melting under the broiling August sun. The tent has raised wooden platforms with an earthen path between them. The platforms serve as our sleeping quarters; that is, each of us is given a straw mat to put on the platform, and that becomes his bed. At night, it is very damp, and so are the straw mats, and, what with the smell of tar and grease and the mildewed, rotting straw mats, the air inside the tent is always stale and nauseating. We have learned to breathe with our mouths open, to avoid, at least, the sickening sensation we get when we inhale or sniff the air through our noses. When it rains, the earthen floor and the path usually get flooded and muddy, and the reddish brown clay stays wet and squishy for several days, giving off a smell that reminds you of rotting fish.

There are about sixty of us in our tent, plus our teacher, a middle-aged Japanese, a scholar on Chinese classics, of all things, who, like the rest of us, sleeps on the straw mat on the platform by the entrance to the tent, though he is separated from us by a bed sheet hung by straw ropes between his bed and the next bed. He could have slept in a tent specially constructed for teachers, but he insisted on sleeping with us, as well as working with us on the field, saying, "We are in this together, aren't we?" In spite of that, he is not popular or respected, though he is not disliked by the class. He has been lately confined to his bed, because he was stricken by a severe case of dysentery. Once a day, he is visited by a Japanese medic, who gave us permission to have someone stay in the tent at all times to look after our teacher. The medic also doles out aspirin tablets and small bags of bitter white powder, which is for diarrhea. Nearly everyone has diarrhea.

Although we suffer from dysentery and diarrhea and chronic indigestion, we can't really complain about our meals—mainly because we do get to have three meals a day. Most of us would be having two meals or, more likely, only one meal a day if we weren't working on a Japanese airfield. Each day, we take turns for "kitchen" duties and take buckets over to the field kitchen and bring back cooked barley and soy-sauce soup that always has bean sprouts or several cubes of bean curd floating in it. As it is about a ten-minute walk from our tent to the field kitchen, our meal is cold by the time we get it to our tent, and, on rainy days, transporting the meal to our tent becomes a major operation. We all have our own utensils, which we brought from home, as well as our own bedrolls.

Speaking of our homes, once a week, for a day, we are allowed either to go home or to have visitors, and most of my classmates, except those who happen to come from nearby towns or villages, learned to stay. What with the shortage of trains and buses, which are now running on charcoal, travel is not only difficult but also demoralizing. If we are late in reporting back to the airfield, we have to do extra work. Some of the well-to-do boys, when they have visitors, manage to get cakes or candies, which become as valuable as money. Although there is a canteen for students by the field kitchen, most of us are without money and try to avoid going to the canteen even if we have money, because the canteen is a favorite gathering place of the Japanese students, who can get things there by using ration coupons while we pay in cash. The Japanese students live apart from the Korean students, in their own tents at the other side of the field, with a cluster of tents for the Japanese airmen between us. We seldom meet one another, even when we are working on the field. We have been here over two months this time.

After work and after our evening meal, which is the same as our breakfast as well as our lunch, though without the

soup, we have classes in our tent. "The school must go on,"
says our principal. So—for two hours a night, ¬der the
dim, flickering halos of kerosene lanterns, we study; that
is, we keep up with the progress of the war, which is supposed to be going very well for Japan, or we read from Japanese history. Having worked all day out on the field in
the hot sun, it is difficult for some of us to stay awake through
the two hours of nightly classes, especially because we have
to kneel and sit on our heels Japanese style on the straw
mat, straining our eyes in the dim light.

"Why don't we quit the school?" we often ask ourselves.
Most of us would have liked to quit the school and go home.
But, getting into the school was difficult to begin with: The
competition was fierce, and, for those of us who came from
small towns and villages, it was doubly difficult to be admitted, and, then, once we quit the school, we would never
be admitted to another high school anywhere in the country
—that is, those who withdraw from the school to avoid "serving the Emperor through labor" become, automatically and
by law, *personae non gratae.* In my own case, I have a special
reason for not quitting; I was told that if I quit the school
while the school is "requisitioned" to work on an airfield or
in a munitions factory, my father would have to give a
report once a week to the local police as to what I was doing
and so forth, like a man out on parole.

*   *   *

This morning, the Japanese corporal who is in charge of
our class inspects our hands and, seeing that my hands are
bubbling and oozing with blisters, orders me to work, along
with eight others, as a gravel-carrier. I and a classmate will,
as a team, go outside the barbed-wire fence (which surrounds
the entire field, including our tents) to a gravel pit worked
on by the students from another high school, load the gravel
into a big straw sack, run a wooden pole through the sack,

and carry it, Chinese-coolie style, to the section of the runway in which our class is digging. Everything is done by
hand; we have not seen a single piece of machinery on the
field, except for a dozen or so stone rollers. Even the cement
that has not been used yet is transported to the field by
oxcarts. When the Kamikaze planes land, they will be the
only machines on the field—if they ever arrive from Manchuria.

I am weak from diarrhea, and I have a splitting headache.
My hands are wrapped in an old towel, which I also use to
wipe the sweat from my face. The sun is glaring hot on our
bare backs, which are blistering and peeling from the heat,
and our shoulders ache and chafe from the weight of the
wooden pole. Our feet are also blistered, and, after a while,
our thin cotton socks get glued to the burning skin of our
feet, and, soon, the rubber soles of our sneakers will stick
to the socks, and our feet will begin to feel as though they
were walking on squishy, wet rubber.

Usually, we manage to start the day laughing and chatting
about what we would like to eat and what we miss most,
which always turns out to be something edible. We have
breakfast at six-thirty, start working at seven-thirty, and, by
nine in the morning, no one is talking very much—until
lunch time comes around.

Around eleven in the morning—I must have made ten or
twelve rounds carrying gravel—the Japanese corporal wants
to see me. The corporal is young, barely twenty, and so thin
that, when he breathes in, you can see the whole of his rib
cage. He, too, is suffering from dysentery or, at least, from
heavy diarrhea; he has a pallid face, yellowish and hollow
around the eyes, as if he hasn't slept for days.

When I report to him, he tells me that my mother has
come to see me. "Visitors are allowed only on Mondays,"
he says, "unless it is for something very urgent, like when
someone dies." He orders another boy to take my place.
He does not seem upset or angry with me, and, as though

he were reciting a regulation for my benefit, he speaks
matter-of-factly. "However, in case of emergency, students
may be allowed to receive visitors at the discretion of the
officer of the day. Permission granted. Make sure you return
to duty as soon as you can. Dismissed." The corporal stands
in front of me, not knowing what else to say or do, panting
and gasping, his naked torso streaming with sweat. He is
actually a college student in his first year who was drafted
as what we call a "quickie" soldier, to be assigned to labor
forces, especially to supervise students working on airfields
or at munitions factories. He is as exhausted and undernourished as anyone else, going through his work me-
chanically. He is so frail and thin that we are not really afraid
of him at all. He is not as strict or mean-tempered as most
of the other Japanese soldiers supervising us; in fact, some
of us suspect that he is more afraid of us than we are of him.
We think—and we have a small bet going—that he is going
to collapse before we do. "All he needs is a little push," says a
wrestler friend of mine, "just a little push." The corporal
shrugs for no apparent reason and gives me his water
canteen. "When you are through, have it filled and bring it
back to me."

I take his canteen, give a little wave of my hand to my
classmates, and head for the main entrance to the airfield.
I pass by a line of my friends who, stripped down to their
waist, are carrying gravel, waddling under the heavy sacks.
They all want to know where I am going and why I am not
working. I tell them that my mother has come to see me. I
move on. The field is swarming with hundreds of students
shoveling, hoeing, removing dirt, carrying gravel . . . and yet
the sizzling field is strangely quiet.

A large tent just inside the main gate is reserved for
visitors. The tent has long wooden tables and benches. On
Monday afternoons, when we are allowed to have visitors,
the tent is packed with parents and relatives, not saying very
much to each other, just looking at each other, the boys

munching on cakes or fruits, some mothers crying quietly and embracing their children when the sergeant of the day comes and announces that the time is up.

The tent is roasting in the sunlight. My mother is standing in the shadow of the tent. She is wearing Japanese-style women's pants, which all women have to wear these days; they are the regulation "uniform" for women, who are not allowed to wear Korean dress outside their homes. My mother looks uncomfortable and terribly out of shape in that baggy and colorless get-up.

I drag one of the wooden benches from inside the tent and place it in the shade. We sit down, side by side, not saying a word for a while. She is holding my hand in her hands. Her fingers are rough, and her fingernails are cracked. She has gotten quite thin lately. She unwraps a small bundle and hands me an apple. I take a bite from it.

"Visitors are not allowed, you know," I say to her, eyeing the Japanese sentry at the gate, "except on Mondays."

"I told them a little lie," she says, trying to smile. She is not successful. Her eyes are filled with tears, watching me munch the apple. She wipes my back with her handkerchief. "Hungry?"

I shake my head. "No."

"I brought you some clean underwear," she says, touching the bundle, "and—this." She takes out white cotton sheets folded into little squares.

"I don't need sheets."

"These are not sheets really. You said you were bothered by bedbugs and insects, so I sewed sheets together, you know, so you can just crawl into them and tie them up around your neck. Won't that help a little?"

I nod. "But how did you get in? What did you tell them? Anything wrong at home?"

"I told them your grandfather is very ill and something like that, and they let me in."

"Which grandfather?"

"Well, both your grandfathers are fine, really. I had to tell them something. I wanted to see you, and then Father thought I should come." She dabs her reddened eyes with the handkerchief.

"Father sent you?"

She looks down for a second. "In a way," she says.

I crush the core of the apple on the dusty ground. "Something is up then," I say.

She hands me another apple. "How is the work going here?" She looks toward the field; hundreds of tiny figures on the field seem hardly to move. "Poor things," she says. "You all have to work like laborers in the sun like this!"

I laugh. "We are laborers, you know."

She shakes her head. "Have you seen any planes yet?"

I laugh again. "That'll be the day. Nothing much is getting done here, you know, and we don't have any machines, like trucks or bulldozers. It'll be a long, long time before any planes can land here."

"It will probably be too late then," she says, lowering her voice a little.

I give her a hard look. "What do you mean?"

"Well, the way the war is going . . ."

"What is the latest news? We don't learn anything new here, except that everything is going all right. Of course, we just don't believe a word of what they say anymore, anyway."

"It won't be long," she whispers, casting a quick glance back to the sentry. "It won't be long at all. That's what Father says."

"He knows something then."

She nods. "Just between us."

Her meaningful look and whispered words make me serious and contemplative, and, for no reason at all, I think of the Japanese corporal whose canteen is dangling by my feet. "No, it won't be long. Even I can tell that." I look at her to emphasize that I am not simply making an idle remark. "A little push, Mother, as we say here. Just a little push—and they will collapse like a man with only skin and bones left."

"Well, they've had that little push already," she says quietly, trying to look casual. "Not many people know about it, though."

By then, I know that my father has something directly to do with her coming to see me and that they are both trying to tell me something. "What happened?"

She takes out of the bundle three cakes of millet with dark sugar. "Germany surrendered a long time ago, almost three months ago, and we were never told about it, of course. And the Russians are attacking the Japanese in Manchuria."

I am too stunned to respond immediately. I only mutter, "In Manchuria . . . the uncle . . ."

"Father was in Manchuria to see your uncle about two weeks ago. They had a talk; so your uncle should be all right."

"The Russians . . ."

"That's not all," she says, her voice hushed. "The Americans have dropped some sort of new bomb on Japan, and the rumor is that it is very powerful, some sort of scientific weapon. One bomb can wipe out a whole city, and Father has heard that two cities have already been destroyed by these bombs. Japan can't last long fighting against that kind of new weapon with bamboo sticks and boys like you slaving on a puny airfield like this."

"It won't be long then. It really won't be long this time."

She nods. "The Americans have landed on Okinawa, too," she says, as though she were saving that piece of information for last. "They have really landed, and it won't be long before they will land in Japan itself. You'll see."

I feel my heart beating wildly, triumphant yet afraid. "When was that!"

"Almost four months ago. How can the Japanese hide that sort of thing from us!"

In my imagination, I see hundreds and thousands of Jap-

anese charging the Americans on the beaches of Okinawa
with bamboo sticks and the American soldiers simply
machine-gunning them down . . . the shovels, the picks, the
straw sacks, the gravel, the barley, and the soy-sauce soup
with bean sprouts, my Japanese teacher down with dysentery, the skinny corporal with hollow eyes, and the Japanese
Kamikaze planes that never showed up. . . .

I look at her. "Does Father want me to come home?"

She says quickly, as though she had been waiting for me
to ask that, "Do you want to?"

"Well, Mother, if it won't be long before the war is going
to be over, I think I'd better come home and stay alert, you
know, just in case. Father would need me around to keep
my eyes open and that sort of thing."

She stares at me in silence, then, with a sniffle, tears shine
in her eyes. "We should all be together, of course," she says.

"Yes, I want to come home," I say firmly. "When the
Japanese are defeated, it will be chaotic everywhere, you
know. For a while, anyway. It may not be easy to travel back
and forth, and who knows when I can ever get home."

Without a word, she takes a piece of paper out of her pants
pocket. She hands it to me.

It is a notice of withdrawal from the school, already
signed by my father.

"Things are pretty urgent then," I say. "It really won't
be long then, if Father feels this way. Why didn't you let
me see this in the first place?"

"We wanted *you* to decide. We didn't want you to feel
that you are running away, you know, deserting your
friends. You are in this together, and you don't want to
look like a weakling, not that slaving for the Japanese is
important or worthwhile. The only thing is that we really
mustn't and can't tell the others. I mean, you simply mustn't
tell your friends why you are quitting. Do you understand
that?"

I nod. "We can't take a chance like that. It is too dangerous."

"It's too bad, but we really can't."

"All right," I say, getting up. "We'd better hurry then. I'll take this to our teacher and tell him I am going home."

"Do you want me to come along?"

"Of course not, Mother. I can handle this. I'll be right back."

She takes out four apples and the three millet cakes I have not touched. "Do you want to give these to your friends?" She wraps them up in a clean towel. "I did bring your clean underwear and the sheets, you know, just in case you didn't think you should quit now."

I take the apples and the cakes. "I'll be back in a minute."

"Will he let you go?"

"I'll just tell him off if he makes a fuss about it."

I run toward our tent. I am going home, I am thinking, I am going home; I am going to quit this rat hole and go home. It won't be long; it won't be long. . . . My running feet raise a cloud of choking red dust, and the sun beats down on my bare back, but I don't mind. I've been waiting for this moment for a long, long time. And now it has come— and I am going home.

The boy who stays with the teacher to look after him is outside the tent, doing laundry, which is one of our duties when we get our turn to stay with the teacher. I tell him to stay outside while I talk with the teacher.

The air is broiling and sickening in the dark tent.

The teacher is sitting cross-legged on his straw mat, reading a magazine, smoking a cigarette. He looks up when I come in. "Oh, it's you," he says, adjusting his thick eyeglasses. He has lost weight, too, I think, as I look at his bony fingers rubbing his nose. "What are you doing here?" he says.

I go up to him and give him the withdrawal notice.

He takes one look at it. "So—," he says, looking me up and

down. He takes off his glasses and bats his eyes a few times. "So—it has come to that."

"Sir?"

"I have always wondered when you would quit."

To my surprise, his tone is neutral and subdued. I am at a loss what to make of his words.

"I am not going to ask you why you are withdrawing from the school at a time like this," he says. "I am only interested in the fact— yes, the fact—that you are, indeed, quitting us."

"Sir, I don't understand you."

"You don't have to say anything," he says, bidding me sit down beside him on the mat. "Now that you are going to leave us, we must have had it. This is the end of us, isn't it?"

I am silent.

He takes a fountain pen from a leather briefcase by his mat and signs the paper. "There," he says, handing it to me. "Now, you can go home."

I don't know what to do or say. I was expecting a tirade from him, and I was determined to have it out with him if he became unpleasant.

He is silent, too, looking past me toward the open entrance, through which he can see the boys working on the field, which shimmers in the sun.

At last, I manage to say, "It is not that I am a weakling and can't take the work . . ."

He quickly interrupts me. "No need to say anything, boy, because I know the real reason for your withdrawal."

His words frighten me a little. I feel uneasy with him. With the paper in my hand, I try to find the proper moment to take leave of him—for good.

Abruptly, he says, "Have you any idea how the war is going?"

I shake my head. "No, sir." Then, quickly, "I mean, sir, everything is going fine."

"You don't have to tell me that, especially you. It is not going well, and you must know that. Don't you? You and

your father must know a way to find out, don't you? And
that's why I have been wondering when you would decide
to go home. You know, I used to tell myself, 'Well, when
that boy quits, we've had it.' "

I squirm, without a sound.

"Don't be afraid of me," he says, smiling. "Not all Japanese are evil men, you know."

"No, sir."

"But you mustn't repeat this to other Japanese."

"I know that, sir."

"We've lost the war," he says in a voice so hushed that
I am awed by it. "To continue the war is sheer lunacy. You
have not seen Japan or Tokyo, of course, but let me tell
you that it is a vast wasteland. Last time I was back home,
it was . . . ah, but why go into that? It is too late. Did you
know or do you know that the Americans have already
landed in Okinawa?"

I remain silent.

"They have," he says. "They landed there a long time
ago."

Without realizing it, I let it slip out of me: "The Russians
have invaded Manchuria. . . ."

"Where did you hear that!"

I say quickly, frightened, "It is just a rumor, sir."

"You must never, never tell that to anyone. Do you understand that? If that is true, then the end has really come.
There is nothing in Manchuria to stop the Russians. You
know there are no planes left there to come all the way
down here and use this airfield! Lots of nonsense! The only
planes left are old primitive ones, unfit for flying. But the
Russians! They have waited this long! Ah—it means troubles.
What dirty, double-crossing opportunists those Russians
are!"

I am afraid of the nature of our conversation and am also
afraid he is getting off the track. "Sir, my mother is waiting."

"She is here?"

"Yes, sir."

"Then you must go. Wait. They may give you trouble at the gate if you show just that withdrawal notice. I'll write out a pass, and you don't have to tell anyone about your withdrawal."

He takes a blank pass and fills it out for me. It says I am going home for three days because of an emergency at home.

"Thank you, sir." I am, to my surprise, really grateful.

He nods. "I suppose you don't understand why I am being kind to you, do you?"

I am touched and say, "I hope you will get better soon, sir. You've lost a lot of weight since we came out here. I do hope everything will be all right for you, sir."

I climb down from the wooden platform and stand on the earthen floor. I bow to him and turn around. I go to my straw-mat bed and collect my things. I leave the apples and cakes on the mat, with a note to my friends to help themselves to them. I wrap up my things in a bed sheet and put them in my bag. I feel the teacher's eyes on my back as I take a step toward the exit, with the bag in one hand and my bedroll in the other. I have to pass by him, and, as I do, I bow to him again, without looking at him.

"Wait a moment," he says.

I feel a big lump in my throat, afraid he may change his mind. "Sir?" I face him.

"Will you remember me?"

Taken aback, I mutter, "Of course, sir."

"Well, your father is a big man in your town, isn't he?"

Bewildered, I don't answer him.

"Oh—I know all about your father."

"Yes, sir?"

"Perhaps—well, I don't quite know how to put it to you," he says, raising his eyes to the tarpaulin ceiling of the rancid tent. The air is hot and suffocating. He lights a cigarette. "Perhaps, one of these days," he says, blowing smoke from his cigarette, "who knows?—I may come to your town."

I don't understand what he is trying to say. "Yes, sir?"

"If I ever come to your town, do you suppose your father would help me?"

I stand silent.

"When we lose the war, we Japanese will have to get out of Korea. That's quite obvious, isn't it? Well, I was just thinking, perhaps your father could help me then. Do you think he would?"

I am now beginning to grasp what is going on between us, and I say, rather boldly, "You mean, sir, like hiding you for a while?"

"What do you think?"

"You won't have to hide from us, sir."

"It may become almost impossible to travel, you know, and anything can happen."

I don't reply.

"You Koreans hate us. I know that in the marrow of my bones."

I keep silent.

"I help you now," he says, smiling, peering at me through his thick glasses, "and you help me later. That's the general idea, you know. What do you think?"

I do not say a word. I know I am not going to reply.

"Please give my regards to your father, will you? And tell him what a fine man I have always thought he is, judging from the way he has brought you up. And you may tell your father what you and I talked about a moment ago. That's quite all right."

I want to get away. I want to run out of the stinking tent, but I don't want to make him angry with me. "I'll tell him that."

"You never know. Perhaps, we'll see each other again before long."

It suddenly strikes me that he is saying this sort of thing

to other boys, too. To a select few . . . just in case. And, with a jolt, I remember several other boys who were given a special pass by him to go home for a few days—and I know the boys well, because we all share one common bond, among others, of having a father who has been convicted for his "Thought Crime," or for his activities in the Independence Movement.

I've got to get out of here, I tell myself. Fast. I bow to him. "Take care of yourself, sir. I may see you again someday."

"Remember me, now," he says, with a smile. "And don't forget! The war isn't over yet, you know."

I am running—away from the tent, away from him, and away from my bondage to their tottering empire. I am running toward my mother. "I'll never see you again," I keep telling myself as I run . . .

. . . but I do see him once more, back in Pyongyang, after our Liberation. . . . I see him working on the streets of Pyongyang, a member of a Japanese labor gang, shoveling and sweeping out the trolley tracks, under the watchful eyes of sullen Russian soldiers in black jackboots with burp guns and German machine pistols. . . . He does not see me, but I see him, and, for one fleeting moment, I am sorry for him, but then I think—For thirty-six years, you and yours have trampled on us and tried to destroy our souls. . . . Love and compassion that have been smothered by the memories of thirty-six years cannot be resurrected by pity that lasts only for a fleeting moment. . . .

My mother is waiting, and I nearly run into her, choking with pounding, aching emotions, trembling with a dizzy swirl of ecstasy and fear. I tell her about the Japanese teacher.

"He must be frightened," she says matter-of-factly. "What do you want to do with this?" She holds out the Japanese corporal's canteen.

I toss it onto the wooden table inside the visitors' tent. "He can get the water himself."

At the gate, I show the pass to a young Japanese private, the sentry. Cradling his rifle, he looks at my pass. He is young, too, not much older than I am. His uniform is soggy with sweat. He gives the pass back to me.

"All right, Boy," he says, tossing his head, eying my mother. "Is someone dying or something?"

I merely nod my head. Yes—someone is dying, I want to shout to him. You and your Empire are dying . . . and I am going home. . . . *I* am going home, *Boy!* . . .

*   *   *

By the dusty, rutted road far from the airfield, we are waiting for a bus . . . and my mother tells me that my maternal grandparents are now at our orchard. My grandfather in Pyongyang, the Presbyterian minister, was put in jail after every Sunday church service, sometimes for a day and sometimes for a few days. A pair of Korean and Japanese Thought Police detectives always came to the Sunday service, taking notes on what my grandfather said in his sermon. Three weeks ago, says my mother, they came and took my grandfather away as usual. He didn't come home for more than a week, and, when he was finally released, everyone could see that he had been beaten. He had cuts on his face and a broken rib. They kept him, my mother says, because they didn't want him to come home until they had patched him up in a hospital. His church, as well as the other Christian churches, was ordered to close down when he was taken away. My parents went to Pyongyang and brought my grandparents to our town.

"They are staying at the cottage," says my mother.

"Is Father staying out there with them, too?"

"No." She puts her hand on my shoulder, drawing me to her. "Don't be afraid," she says. "They took your father away to a detention camp." She begins to sob. "Four days ago," she says.

In the Making
of History — Together

It is the middle of August, and although the height of the rainy season in our region has come and gone, it is still raining on and off, sometimes in the morning, sometimes in the afternoon—a sudden, quick downpour, with the roll of thunder drumming and flashes of lightning bayoneting out of billowy black rain clouds. Then, as suddenly as it comes, the rain will stop, and the dark clouds will drift away. The brilliant, sizzling sun will appear in the clear blue sky, and the air will be filled with the pungent odors of muddy earth, wet trees, shrubs, flowers, and thatched roofs drying, rendering our town steaming and shimmering in the white heat of the sun. And, again, a black rain cloud will loom up on the horizon, quickly seizing and gripping other clouds in the darkening sky, towering up and up like a giant, clenched fist rising and rising, and, when it hovers above our town, it will burst open and let loose a deluge so heavy and thick that you almost think you can count each pellet of rain.

But, this morning, there is no rain, and the morning air— a thin, viscous mist—hangs motionless, low above the earth.

My father is still being kept at the detention camp thirty miles west of our town, where all the politically suspect Koreans have been detained by the Japanese Military Police and the Thought Police. My mother and sisters and my little brother are all out in the orchard. I am alone in the house with my grandparents. I would have been at the orchard, too, had it not been for our doctor's order. When I came home from the student labor camp, my diarrhea became worse and developed into a mild case of dysentery, and the doctor wanted me to stay in town so that he could see me regularly; he had also declared that I was suffering from malnutrition, though there was nothing anyone could do about that.

"Is it twelve o'clock yet?" my grandfather asks, standing in the courtyard.

"In a few minutes, Grandfather."

He comes over and sits down on the edge of the veranda outside my room. "You'd better turn the radio on," he says, removing his shoes. He sits cross-legged on the floor of the veranda. "The police said yesterday to listen to the radio today. At noon. Some important announcement—whatever it may be."

Yesterday, the police were out in force, going around the town, reminding everyone to listen to the radio because the Japanese Emperor was going to make a very important announcement about the war. The Emperor was going to say something about "a fantastic new weapon" invented by Japan, a policeman was supposed to have said to some people in our neighborhood—a new weapon so awesome and miraculous that it will surely wipe out the Americans in no time— or something about the "decisive battle on the mainland," and so forth.

My grandfather is sitting next to me when I bring the radio out to the veranda and turn it on. He can't understand a word of Japanese, so I will translate for him. He has never been to school, but he has taught himself to read—to read Korean, that is—and he has always read daily papers in Korean, but there hasn't been a single newspaper in Korean for some time; that is, the Japanese have banned the newspapers printed in Korean.

First, amid the crackling static, the dirgelike Japanese national anthem is played; then the voice of the Emperor (so we were told yesterday, having never heard the Emperor's voice before) comes out of the radio. We were reminded yesterday that, when his voice is heard on the radio, we must all face the radio and touch the floor with our heads as we sit on our knees. Listening to the Emperor's invocation of the "sacred names" of his "divine ancestors," I sit cross-legged as my grandfather does.

"Well, what is he saying?" he asks, looking out to the courtyard, which is hazy with the sun. "Has he said anything important yet?"

I shake my head, tuning the dial of the radio. Then, I sit up straight, jolted by what I am hearing, raising the volume of his voice . . . and, overwhelmed by the stunning, unbelievable message of the Emperor, beside myself with a choking excitement and the pounding of my heart, I am standing up, not knowing how to control myself, trying to tell my grandfather that the Emperor is saying that Japan is surrendering to the Allied powers unconditionally, but my voice is breaking, and I am simply throwing myself onto him, sobbing.

My grandmother hurries out to the veranda, saying, "What's the matter? What's going on? Why is he crying?"

I scream out that Japan has surrendered to the Americans.

My grandmother stares at me for a moment, then she goes down on her knees by the radio, her wrinkled hands outstretched toward my grandfather, who sits there unmoving, silent, gazing up into the cloudless blue sky of the sizzling August day. My grandmother clutches at his arms and begins to cry openly, trying to say something.

Suddenly, my grandfather breaks down, with a great sob,

and tears stream down his face, down to his long white beard. He, too, can't control himself and he pulls me to him, hugging me, stroking me, saying, between his sobs, "Oh, your father! Oh, your father!"

My grandmother grips my hands, weeping. "If they killed your father . . . if they killed him!"

Feeling as if I am going out of my mind, I shout, "If they killed him, I'll kill every single Japanese in town!"

The Emperor's voice is droning on over the radio—telling why he decided to surrender and how he is ashamed of himself before his heavenly ancestors. . . . I shut his voice off.

I turn to my grandfather. "I swear, I'll kill every Japanese in town if they killed my father. I swear, I swear!"

My grandfather, now composed, pulls me up and leads me to his room. "Bring me a big knife!" he tells one of the maids in the kitchen.

With the long knife in his hand, he goes to the wall where there is a built-in cabinet. He plunges the knife into the wall directly below the cabinet and cuts out the wallpaper and the plaster beneath it. The wall has a hollow space. He puts his hand into the hollow and takes out a package wrapped tightly with oiled paper. He cuts the wrapping open. A small wooden box emerges.

Inside the box are small packets, also wrapped in oiled paper. He opens one packet and takes out a flag neatly folded into a small square. It is the flag of Korea. Other packets contain some documents and military insignia—in his youth, before the Japanese occupation, my grandfather was a sergeant in the old Royal Army of Korea. He stands up, with the flag in his hands. He gives it to me, saying, "It's yours now. Go and fly it."

I run out through the east gate and take down the flag pole that still flies the Japanese flag. Every house had to fly the Japanese flag every day. . . . I run back into the house with the flag pole, with the Japanese flag still tied to it. My grandfather cuts the Japanese flag off the pole. My grandmother picks the flag up, goes into the kitchen, and says to the maids, "Burn it."

We tie the Korean flag to the pole and go out to the east gate and put the pole up. He stands by the flag pole for a moment, then he grips the pole impulsively, shouting across the street, "Come on out, everyone! We are free! We are independent! Come on out, all of you! We'll celebrate! By heavens, we'll celebrate!"

*   *   *

It is one o'clock in the afternoon. A great many people are coming and going, in and out of our house. A crowd is filling the courtyard. They are looking for my father. A number of young men in a group, having been told that my father's fate is unknown, are saying that they should storm the police station, capture the weapons, and race to the detention camp. Some urge caution. Then someone shouts, "Let's go and burn down the goddamn shrine!" And someone else shouts, "It's already burning!"

Everyone rushes out of the house through the west gate. Outside the house, we can see the mountain behind it. Smoke is rising from the mountain. "There it goes!" people shout. "Let's go and see it!" Everyone dashes up the hill toward the mountain. I follow them out, but my grandfather wants me to come back into the house.

My grandmother is in the kitchen, preparing our lunch. She wants to cook everything we have in the storeroom. She and the maids are bustling around. "We're going to have a lot of people coming and going," my grandmother is saying, "and we are going to feed everyone!"

I tell my grandfather that I will run outside the house and see what is going on in town.

Every street, every road, every alley is packed with people, waving flags, singing, shouting, greeting each other, everyone. Noises and sounds of all kinds fill the air—drums, bugles, whistles, buckets, pots and pans, bells . . . the whole town is exploding with ecstasy, vibrating the hot air. Waves of the crowd surge in and out of the street, at every corner, staging impromptu demonstrations. In the open-air market place, bamboo sticks, wooden rifles, and Japanese flags are piled high and set on fire. Japanese war posters and slogans are methodically ripped off every wall and every telephone pole. Someone is shouting that a huge crowd has gathered in front of the police station. "Let's go!" shouts someone, and the crowd stampedes toward the police station. Every Japanese house is closed tight and silent. Stores owned by the Japanese are also closed. A young man screams above the other voices, "Let's smash them down!" Another young man says, "Come on! Let's take them!" A middle-aged man, waving a thick stick, shouts, "But don't touch any of their filthy stuff! Don't let them say we looted them!" But his voice gets lost in the deafening roar of the crowd. Stones fly in the air, smashing windows. People tear down all the Japanese signs from shops and stores. All the Japanese flags, too.

Down the main street, a small band is blaring out music, and a big crowd is dancing in the middle of the street. I can't see the people playing the music. Boom—Boom go their drums, and the rippling notes of their bugles and the clanging of their brass cymbals sing out. Children are running around, mingling with the grown-ups, dodging them, circling them. Everyone is laughing.

Dazed, I move around, greeting people I know, shouting to my friends, simply making noise. The people who recognize me keep asking me, "Is your father home yet? What do you know about your father? Is he safe?"

And, with the thought of my father suddenly seizing me and making me shake with fear, I run back to the house.

My grandfather and our young farmer have spread a large straw mat on the courtyard by the flower bed and set up a few tables. Bottles of wine and cups are on the table. My grandfather is downing wine, saying to me, "You, too!"

I can hear gongs and drums echoing from the mountain, now and then blending with the thunderous rumbling of the crowd at the burning shrine.

I hear someone calling my father's name in Japanese.

"Who is that!" my grandfather roars.

It is the Japanese Shinto priest next door, calling my father's name through the bamboo fence.

"What does he want?" my grandfather asks me, frowning.

I take a step toward the fence, when the bald-headed priest cuts the ropes that hold the bamboo fence up and he stumbles into our courtyard. Through the opening in the fence, I catch a glimpse of his fat wife crouching on the ground, peering into our house. The priest gets up on his bare feet. He is wearing gray pants and a white shirt. I have never seen him wearing anything other than his priest's kimono.

My grandfather says, "Get out of my house!"

The priest doesn't understand Korean. He keeps bowing his bald head and slides toward us, going up to my grandfather. "Please help us! Please help us!" he is saying.

"What's he babbling about?" says my grandfather.

I say to the priest, "You'd better get out of our house!"

He turns to me. "Please help us! I must speak to your father! He'll help us."

Enraged, I scream, "My father is in your detention camp! He may have been killed by your Military Police! And here you are asking us to help you!"

Suddenly, he goes down on his knees, his palms pressed together in front of him. "The mob! The mob is coming down the mountain! They will kill us! Please help us!" He kowtows, touching his shiny head to the ground. "Please! We know you are a decent family, Christian, and your father would have helped us. Please let us hide in your father's house. The mob—they won't look for us in your house. Please!"

I tell my grandfather what the priest has said.

My grandmother, flanked by the two young maids, says, "I don't want my house defiled by that witchcraft man. Tell him to get out!"

The young farmer steps up to the priest.

My grandfather holds him by the arm. "What do you think we should do?" he says to me.

Taken aback by his question—more surprised by his asking my opinion on the matter—I say to him, "Grandfather! You are asking me?"

I look down on the Japanese. The priest is immobile at my feet, his forehead and hands pressed to the ground, kneeling, muttering, "I beg you, I beg you."

I command all the cold-bloodedness within me. "Of all the people in town, you dare come to us. Do you know anything about my father? Do you know who he is!"

"Yes, yes. I am sorry."

"And still you come to us to ask us to hide you! Why don't you ask your gods to help you? Well, your gods are being burnt down. I ask you, in my father's name, to get out of this house."

"I understand you well. But your father would have helped us. Your father is a good man, a decent man, a kind Christian. He would have helped us. We Japanese have talked about your father before, many times, and we all knew that, when a day like this came, your father would be the only person in town we could count on. Please!"

With that, he raises himself, and, still on his knees, he stuffs his hand into his pants pocket and takes out something wrapped in white rice paper. He holds it in both hands. "Please! Take this. Gold. All we have. Please. We'll never forget your help. Take it. Take it!"

I am trembling, and my voice is shaking. "We do not want your filthy gold!"

Not hearing me, he unwraps the paper. His hands are jerky, and his fingers fumble.

I scream, "Put that away!"

He clutches the paper, and everything in his hands, looking up at me in shock.

I look into his small eyes. Dazed, frightened eyes, bloodshot and glazed.

He bows to me, flipping his head down and up, like a mechanical doll.

I look away.

My grandmother goes back into the kitchen with the maids. "Get him out," she says, as she goes.

My grandfather stands quietly for a moment, then he strides to the tables on the straw mat and pours the wine into a cup. He drains it down. He looks into the empty cup for a second, and, abruptly, with a roar, he smashes it against the stone walk, and marches off into the house.

"Grandfather!" I call after him.

He stops, without turning around. "That man knows your father only too well," he says. "Your father would have saved them! We don't even know whether or not he is alive—and there that man. . . . Boy, you are the man in your family. Your father isn't here, so you take care of it." He stomps into the house and slams the door shut behind him as he goes into his room.

Gongs and drums and cymbals are sounding louder now, shaking the mountain. The roar of the crowd on the mountain is getting louder, too.

With a whine, the priest's fat wife slides through the opening in the bamboo fence and thumps down to our yard.

The priest leaps up, goes to her, and picks her up.

They clutch at each other, looking back toward their house. They turn around to me.

"Please," she says, bowing to me. "Please!"

She, too, is barefoot, in a gaudy kimono, disheveled.

Without shame, they fling themselves down on their knees before me, bowing deeply. "Save us, please! We beg of you!"

I avert my eyes from their sight, and, as I do so, tears come to my eyes.

I look down on them. The priest's shaven head, its center shiny and smooth, without a strand of hair, his thin, pale neck, his flappy ears—and his swarthy fat wife, her rumpled hair graying at the temples, her enormous rear, her dirty heels . . . and I am thinking of the day in the blizzard, at the shrine, of how the priest, resplendent in his silks, called my "Japanese" name, bowing toward where his emperor was supposed to be . . . and of the shrine now burning in flames in the mountains. . . .

"Get up," I say to them, turning my face away. "My father would have saved you."

"Thank you. We are sorry," they chant in unison. "We'll never forget your kindness."

"In that air-raid shelter," I tell them. "Hide in there until we call you. No one will come to our house looking for you."

They get up, bowing and bowing, the priest's wife weeping, sliding backward from me.

I tell the young farmer to get them inside the air-raid shelter, cover it up, and fix the bamboo fence so that the opening won't be noticed.

"I don't know, I don't know," he says, shaking his head. "I guess your father would have done the same, but I don't like it. If people find out about this . . ."

"You don't have to tell them."

"All right, all right."

A little while later, the mob, having come down from the mountain where the shrine is still burning, now with drums and gongs and cymbals beating an eerie cadence in the blazing hot mid-afternoon sun, descends on the priest's Japanese-style house and smashes it. Alone in the courtyard, I hear the clanging and jangling of glasses breaking, the ripping and cracking of doors, paper screens, and furniture being demolished—and the footsteps of the voiceless mob. I hear chairs, tables, and all that is in the house thrown out and piled outside on the road. "Burn them!" someone commands. "The son of a bitch must be hiding in the police station! Burn them! Burn the ghosts down!"

I leave the courtyard, feeling my throat dry and my body trembling, turning away from the unseen presence of the priest and his woman huddled in the dank darkness of the air-raid shelter. I feel neither angry nor ennobled—just a little sad, though without knowing why.

*   *   *

It is sometime after four o'clock in the afternoon. I am standing in the shadow of the evergreens in the courtyard, watching my father in my grandfather's room. He is on his knees, with head bowed before my grandfather, who is holding my father's hands. I see my grandmother coming into the room. She is going down on her knees, too, edging toward my father, and she is putting her hand on my father's shoulder. I can't hear their voices, but I can see their faces—their faces streaming with tears. I can see my father's shoulders heaving. My grandmother is taking out a handkerchief from the inside of her left sleeve and she is drying her face, then she is passing the handkerchief to my father. With arms crossed in front of me, standing alone there in the shadow, I am letting my own tears run down my cheeks, gazing at the reunion inside my grandfather's room through the mist of my tears. My father has just come home. . . .

On that day, my father, still confined in the detention camp, manages to hear from his contact outside the camp that the Japanese Emperor has broadcast Japan's surrender. Fearing the worst, my father and several others quickly organize their fellow inmates, about one hundred and seventy Koreans, and pass the word out to their men outside the camp to mobilize a large crowd nearby. They resolve to fight if the Japanese detachment guarding the camp intends to carry out its contingency plan, which is to shoot everyone in the camp. Outside the camp, our men are gathering weapons, pistols and rifles, some that have been hidden and some that have been captured from Korean policemen fleeing from the villages to which they had been assigned. The men intend to smuggle weapons into the camp; a battle plan is drawn up.

At a signal from inside the camp, both the crowd outside and the inmates inside will overpower the Japanese guards and storm the detachment headquarters. Sharpshooters are assigned to kill the soldiers manning the gate. When the time comes to attack, the inmates will set a fire in one of the buildings. The crowd outside is facing, through the barbed-wire fence, the Japanese soldiers, who have rifles fixed with bayonets.

Soon after the crowd has gathered outside, a Japanese corporal, who is the commandant's orderly, comes to my father and the others and says, very politely—he is frightened and bewildered—that the commandant wishes to see my father and a few other Koreans at his quarters. There is a quick conference, and it is decided that they will go and see the commandant. My father announces that he will tell the commandant that, if anything happens to them, the camp will come under attack.

My father and the others are shown into the commandant's private quarters. There, in the presence of his officers, the commandant, a young major of the Imperial Army, dressed not in his uniform but in a kimono, orders his officers to release the Koreans immediately and to take the detachment back to their regimental headquarters in Pyongyang, where they will disarm themselves and await the arrival of the Russians.

Then—in full view of everyone—he commits hara-kiri: He plunges a small ceremonial sword into the left side of his underbelly, slits it open, and orders his deputy to cut his head off. The commandant's head is severed from his body with a large sword by his deputy, a young captain. A moment after the major's head has rolled to the matted floor of the room, the captain, sitting by the crumpled body of the major, shoots himself in the temple. Other officers, all very young, blood-spattered, dazed, and nearly delirious, stumble out of the quarters into the blinding sunlight, mute and frightened.

The crowd outside the camp is becoming larger and larger. Silence prevails. The inmates are out by their barracks, hushed, watching my father and the others, also blood-spattered, coming out of the commandant's quarters. The Japanese officers are huddled together, five of them, not knowing what to do. My father and the others take charge of the detention camp and announce that Japan has surrendered to the Allied powers, that the inmates are to go home immediately, and that they themselves are taking over the detention camp. They then tell the Japanese officers to please disarm themselves and their men and turn the weapons over to the Koreans. The Japanese detachment is quickly disarmed and is sent off to Pyongyang in the camp's trucks. The captured weapons are turned over to the local committee of public safety. My father goes from the camp to his friend's house, borrows a bicycle, and comes home. . . .

I can see . . . I am seeing my grandfather turning and looking out to the courtyard where I am standing, and I am hearing his voice, "Why don't you come inside?" And I am seeing all their faces turned to me, smiling.

But I am not moving, remaining in the deep shadows of the evergreens by the flower bed, my heart filled with silent joy and pride, smiling back, watching the three of them together. I am closing my eyes, as if to etch their figures onto the brilliant multicolored plate of my memory as I am lifting my face toward the blue sky gleaming with sun. I am opening my eyes and I am seeing my father emerging from the room and coming toward me—slowly, slowly—and he is standing beside me, putting his arm around my shoulders. I am touching his thin hand, his rough, bony hand, and his arm and, looking up, I am seeing his face, his emaciated face with those hollow eyes that are filling up with silent tears. I am seeing his face twitching and struggling as he is trying to hold back his tears and smile. Out of the corner of my eye, I am seeing my grandfather and my grandmother, blurry figures in white, coming out of the room and standing on the veranda looking at us, and I am burying my face into my father, smelling the starch of his clean clothes and the soap and himself; I am feeling his arms around me tighten and hearing his voice saying, "I am going out to the orchard, and you are coming along with me."

I am nodding my head, letting him slowly lead me out of the shadows of the evergreens to the veranda, where my grandparents are standing. I am sitting down on the edge of the veranda, between my father and my grandmother, and I am feeling my grandmother's hand on my shoulder, and she is wiping my face with her handkerchief, which is wet. I am listening to my father's voice saying to my grandfather, "There is a rumor that a Japanese regiment has mutinied in Pyongyang, not wanting to surrender. It is tense everywhere, and we must be very careful. We can't take a chance right now. We've got to get organized and take the initiative away from the local Japanese."

I am saying, "We won't let the Japanese push us around any longer, will we, Father? We will fight, won't we?"

He is saying, "We will. We will. We will have to arm ourselves and disarm the Japanese, at least in our own town."

My grandfather is saying, "Do you still have that pistol?"

"It is out in the orchard," my father is saying.

"What pistol?" I am saying.

"Your uncle brought one for me sometime ago. It is buried in the orchard. Some of my friends and our people have hunting rifles hidden away, but that is not enough. We've got to take over the police."

"I was going to kill every Japanese in town, if anything happened to you."

"I know, but we are not going to kill anyone. Do you understand that? We will arm ourselves not to kill the Japanese but to defend ourselves if they mean to do any harm to us."

"We will fight them, won't we, Father?"

"If we are attacked."

"Do you think they will do anything?"

"I don't know. We will soon find out. Judging from the way it was at the detention camp, I doubt it. But I don't like the sound of this rumor about that mutiny. I hope it is not true."

My grandmother is saying, "You two had better get going."

My grandfather is saying, "I'll keep my eyes open here and let you know what is going on. You'd better stay put in the orchard, just in case."

My father is getting up from the veranda, saying to me, "Come on. Let's go now. We have lots to do."

The shadows of the evergreens are lengthening in the ripe afternoon sun, and the courtyard is half-covered with the shadows. A big dragonfly is sailing in the air over the flower bed.

"You'd better go quickly, before anyone finds out you are back," my grandfather is saying.

My father is getting his bicycle. I am already on mine, watching the dragonfly darting around. Then, I am remembering the Japanese Shinto priest and his wife in the air-raid shelter. I am laughing and laughing.

"Father," I am calling. "Father! The shrine-keeper and his wife! In the air-raid shelter!"

My grandparents have forgotten about them, as I had.

My grandfather explains it to my father.

"Give them something to eat," my father is saying, "and keep them in there till I am back."

"I did it for your sake," I am saying to my father.

He is smiling at me. "I would have done the same for your sake." He is getting onto his bicycle. "Let's go."

"Yes, sir. Anything you say, sir!"

And I see myself bouncing on the seat as though riding on a horse, pedaling away, gripping the handle bars, laughing and laughing, not crying any more, keeping up with my father, bursting with the joy of seeing him alive and of being alive, now shooting my bicycle ahead of his, feeling his smile and gaze on my back like the warm afternoon sun, looking back to him, shouting, "Come on, Father!"

*   *   *

". . . For thirty-six years, Lord, for thirty-six long years, we have been praying for this day," my mother is praying, "and the day has come at last. You have blessed us with our freedom this day, Lord, and you have returned our beloved, the father of our children, to us safe and unharmed. Lord, keep us in your grace and guide us in this uncertain time. For thirty-six long years, we have looked for your love and blessing and guidance, always looking for your sign, keeping our faith in you, Lord, and we pray for your wisdom and continued guidance as we step toward the unknown, toward the tomorrow in our new life. You have graced us with our country's salvation and with our family's salvation, and, when we look back on those years of darkness and persecution, when we look back on those . . ."

My mother's voice breaks down, and, fighting her sobbing, she covers her face with her hands. My maternal grandparents, my sisters clinging to my father, and my baby brother by my mother . . . their heads bowed, my sisters sobbing now, my brother crawling up onto my mother's lap—and I am sitting quietly, my eyes open, and I am saying:

"We are not going to cry anymore."

And my grandfather, his eyes closed, continues my mother's prayer, ". . . . When we look back on those years of darkness, we are ashamed of those moments of our weakness when we gave in to our despair, oblivious of your presence among us

in time of joy and sorrow, overcome as we were by the forces
of evil and persecution. And here we are gathered together,
Lord, this day of our liberation, and we offer you our thanks
and prayers for having sustained us in body and spirit. Lord,
oh, Lord . . . Amen."

Everyone is silent for a while. My mother's eyes are puffed
and red. My sisters are at my father's sides, basking in his
presence. My grandfather shakes my father's hand. My
grandmother takes my baby brother from my mother, whose
eyes are welling with tears again. Outside the cottage, farmers
and their wives are gathering, waiting for my father.

I say to my father, "Come on, Father. We've got lots of
things to do. I want to see that pistol. Let's go and dig it
up."

My mother hushes me; I don't care. I am thinking of
organizing our farmers. We must post sentries, maybe five or
six of them, along the dirt road from the orchard to the
main road. One sentry on top of the mountain behind the
orchard, too. We must set up a system of relaying information, send someone to the town every hour on the hour,
pass the word around to my father's friends that he is back
at the orchard, that they should organize themselves, too,
and that, perhaps, they should all get together quickly. We
must post lookouts here and there to watch for any troop
movement on the main road from the direction of Pyongyang, and we should also mobilize the townspeople and all the
young men in the neighboring villages and . . .

My father says, "All right. Let's get to work."

"Yes, sir!" When we are away from the family, I say to him,
"Well, aren't you glad I am home to help you, Father?"

He merely smiles.

"Here's what I think we should do . . ." I am saying.

*   *   *

The giant red sun is still hovering over the ridges of the

towering mountains behind our orchard, casting a line of deep shadow that is slowly advancing over the expanse of apple trees as the sun is gradually sinking in the west. Half of the orchard is immersed in the shadow, with the other half still glowing warm—green, yellow, and orange. From the terrace of our cottage, I can see the dirt road leading out of the orchard all the way to the small village about two miles from the main road. I see puffs of dust on the dirt road around the bend just outside the village. Someone is bicycling up toward the orchard. It must be someone we know, because our men posted along the road, to keep an eye open for any sort of unusual movement or activity, would have sent a boy running to us if it were a stranger on the road.

I am oiling and polishing the pistol, a small-caliber automatic made in Russia, which my father and I have dug up from the earth near an apple tree in the middle of the orchard. It was heavily greased and wrapped in oiled paper and canvas. There are two magazines of bullets for the pistol. We need more weapons; so far, we have only one pistol, one shotgun, also dug up from its hiding place, and an air rifle, fit only for shooting birds, though it is better than nothing, as the man who brought it out with him said rather sheepishly.

"Can he handle that thing?" asks a man, watching me disassemble the pistol.

"Probably better than I can," says my father.

I don't want to show off. I merely smile at the men gathered around the terrace. Thirteen, fourteen men have come out to the orchard in the late afternoon, one by one, so as not to arouse anyone's curiosity, everyone on a bicycle. Sure, I can handle any weapons, I want to tell them. Give me anything, including a light machine gun and light mortar, and I will show you how to shoot them.

"Let's face it," says the man who is cradling the shotgun. "He's probably the only one among us who has some kind of military training, thanks to the Japanese."

"He ought to start organizing our army," says another.
They laugh and go back to discussing how best to take
over the police station and other government offices. They
have been arguing over tactics and priorities, and so forth,
some too excited, some overly cautious, and some simply not
knowing how to deal with a situation such as this, that is, the
taking over of power, something that none of them has ever
experienced or even dreamed of.

I am listening to their discussion quietly—on the side line,
so to speak—still keeping my eyes on the dirt road. I can't
see the figure on the bicycle but I know someone is coming
up the road. The grown-ups' idea of fighting a "war" seems
so naïve that, trying to catch my father's attention, I edge
toward their circle. They seem afraid mainly that the
Japanese policemen will decide to "retaliate" and "put up a
last-ditch fight" rather than lay down their arms as they
have been ordered to do by the Emperor. I decide that the
adults are too cautious and have no understanding of such
tactics as isolating your enemy or dividing their forces or
mounting flanking attacks or even ambushing them, and so
forth. I am becoming a little impatient with their delibera-
tions. I step up to my father's side, trying to look incon-
spicuous as I whisper to him, "You are not really covering
the whole battlefield, sir."

He looks at me with his head tilted, and a faint smile
appears on his face. "Any bright ideas?" he says.

I glance at the other men to gauge their willingness to
listen to me.

"Well?" says the man with the shotgun.

"I think you are worrying about the police too much,"
I say, lowering my eyes as if I am reluctant to speak out in
the middle of their adult discussion. "I wouldn't worry about
them at this stage, if I were you."

"Go on," says my father.

I look around to see if anyone is displeased with my inter-
ference. To my surprise, everyone seems to be interested in

what I have to say. I quickly conclude that they have, indeed, been worrying too much about what the police would or might do—a negative, passive, tactical kind of thinking, rather than exploring ways and means by which they can destroy the police or at least neutralize them. Emboldened, I go on: "The police can be isolated, sir. Most of them are inside the station right now, anyway. We should try to keep them in there and just make sure they don't come out in force. We can always deal with two or three of them at a time, but I doubt if the police will be stupid enough to send anyone out at a time like this. There are Korean policemen, too, sir, and we should talk them into coming out and giving themselves up. But, sir, really, the first thing we should do is to take over everything else, that is, the railway station, the fire department, the government warehouses, and that sort of thing. Cut the telephone wires to and from the police station, cut off their water by locating the water pipes to the station and destroying them, cut off the electric supply, and so on. Then surround the station and send in an ultimatum, asking them to lay down their arms and turn the station over to us. It is really very simple, sir."

My father keeps smiling, not saying a word. The others are quiet, too.

Encouraged by their receptivity, I continue, "We need weapons, sir. We'll have them when we take over the police station, but, even before that take-over, we can get the weapons. We should organize the townspeople and send a large crowd to every Japanese house in town. I am sure no one will put up a fight if we have a big crowd at each house. We search the house, take whatever weapons we can find, and have all the Japanese civilians in town gather somewhere, like in the school auditorium or the town theater."

"Like hostages, you mean?" says my father. "A detention camp?"

"Why not, sir?" I say.

He is silent.

"I wouldn't say it is a detention camp if I were you, sir. What the Japanese tried to do was to shoot you, sir. I don't think you should forget that. But what we are trying to do is simply to collect all the Japanese civilians, mainly to isolate them from the police—first, to minimize the number of Japanese men available to the police, second, to protect the Japanese civilians from some of our own people. Who knows, sir? Anything can happen. Some of our people may do something extreme and terrible to some Japanese and that may trigger the Japanese police."

"Well, so, what if the police charge out?" says a man.

"We will have surrounded the station by then, sir. That's why we should act immediately. We should find any kind of explosives, dynamite, for example. We can even organize a group of archers, you know, sir, with fire arrows like in the old days. Also, we can bring all the fire trucks with water hoses. Better than nothing, sir. If it comes to the worst, we can always burn down the station. Set up barricades, too, sir, around the station and also on all the roads in and out of our town. But the first thing really is to cut off telephone, electricity, and water to the station."

"You have a real anarchist in your family!" says a man to my father, chuckling.

"You've got to organize the people first, sir," I say. "Organize them quickly because, right now, our people are simply a crowd, a mob. You've got to organize them and assign them specific targets, like the railway station, warehouses, and so on. We should round up everyone who knows how to handle weapons, and have them organized into a sort of battle group. It is all very simple, really, sir. But you've got to go back into the town and take the initiative, sir, before the people get too confused or too excited, or before the Japanese get too desperate and frightened, if you know what I mean, sir. Someone's got to lead the people, and you've got to take that leadership, sir."

Before anyone can say anything, I quickly excuse myself from the group and move away from the terrace.

The man on a bicycle is coming up the path. It is our doctor. He parks the bicycle and comes up to the terrace.

"How is your stomach?" he says, smiling. "Feel better?"

"I've forgotten about it, sir," I say. "No time to think about it."

"Well, I can imagine," he says, mopping his brows with a handkerchief. "What are they doing?"

"Talking, sir."

He gives me a wink. "Talking, talking, I am sure."

I shrug my shoulders and escort him to the group.

"He's been lecturing us on military tactics," says my father, shaking hands with the doctor. "What is the town like now?"

"It is tense, as you can imagine," he says, removing his white jacket and his straw hat. His white shirt is stuck to his back, wet. "The police haven't made any move. They are still inside the station and, as far as I know, no one has seen a single policeman in town. I am sure they are talking and talking, too, and trying to get in touch with their people elsewhere."

"What about the people?" someone asks.

"Everywhere. Just milling around. Someone ought to do something. On my way out here, I saw hundreds of people from the villages coming into the town. They want to know what's going on in town. Pretty soon, the whole town is going to be packed with people, and who knows what can happen."

"We've got to do something quickly," says the man with the shotgun. "We were going over that before you came."

"All right," says my father. "Let's decide on the committee formation and then we can go over the details."

With that, he dismisses me from the group.

I go inside the cottage and into the kitchen, where my mother is preparing meals for the men.

"I heard you talking to the grown-ups," she says, peeling cucumbers. "Aren't you a bit too forward?"

I shrug my shoulders. "They've been talking and talking all this time—wasting time, if you ask me. They've got to do something soon, before the situation in town gets out of hand. A mob may try to storm the police station, and a lot of people may get hurt. Besides, someone else or another group may try to take the leadership away from Father's group."

"Well, I don't like all this talk about guns and so on, especially you with that pistol and talking like a soldier."

"But, Mother, the men out there don't know anything. That generation, Mother, is too scared and too timid."

"They've survived so far, haven't they?" says my mother sharply. "They ought to be given some credit for that."

"Is survival everything, Mother?"

"It kept all of us alive to this day."

There is very little one can say to that sort of argument— I think. I am getting impatient with everyone. "You know what grandfather said in his prayer. . . ."

"Yes?"

"I am not ashamed of anything he is ashamed of. What I am really ashamed of is that our liberation was given to us, Mother. We didn't get it ourselves. It just dropped from the sky. Just like that. A present! That's what we ought to be really ashamed of."

She looks at me for a moment. Then she laughs. "You sound just like your father before he married me."

"What is that supposed to mean?"

She gives me a slice of cucumber. "You'll understand someday."

"Why is it that everything has to be understood later— someday?"

"Because you are still a little boy. That's why."

"I am not a little boy any more, Mother. Today, I put an end to that stage of my life. I am thirteen years old, you know."

She gives me an exaggerated bow. "Whatever you say, Master!"

"Oh, come on, Mother!"

Munching the cucumber, I stalk out, with the pistol in my hand.

*   *   *

All the men are now gone, one by one, to meet later at our house in town. The committee for self-rule and public safety has been formed and my father is its chairman. Everyone has been assigned a specific task. It has been decided to take over the railway station so as to control the rail traffic, to occupy the government warehouses so as to take over supplies and grain and distribute them to our people, and to requisition every available bus and truck in order both to transport the people from the neighboring villages to the town and to dispatch detachments to occupy the town's water depot, electric-transformer station, and minor government offices, as well as the fire department. The local telephone office is inside the police station; so it is decided to cut the telephone wires leading to and from the station immediately. Unfortunately, the cutting of the telephone wires will also deprive us of our own means of communication with the world outside our town; we have to devise a system of relaying information, using five or six men with bicycles, between our town and the neighboring towns, which are fifteen miles to the north, twenty miles to the south, and thirty miles to the west.

The town is to the east of our orchard and, as my father and I, just the two of us, pedal along the main road toward the town, the twilight sun casts long shadows ahead of us on the road, dancing and ever lengthening. On both sides of the road, the farmers from the outlying villages are moving toward the town—some on oxcarts but most of them on foot. The word has already gone out to all the villages to turn out in force and gather in the town at the open-air market place, which is several blocks from the police station. Many farmers recognize my father, and there is a constant exchange of greetings as we move along. The top of the mountain behind our house in town is glowing red with the scarlet setting sun, and, below it, the town is indistinct with the gathering darkness and the blue-gray haze. At the bridge just outside the town, my father wants to take a detour to avoid going through the main street. We turn to the right at the end of the bridge, which stands over the swollen, roaring river, and ride on the bank along the river. The bank will come to an end at the foot of the school field, and, from there, a dirt road will meander through several clusters of houses and come out behind our house.

My father does not say much, until we are on the last stretch of the road, before we can see our house. "Your mother told me what you said to her," he says then, motioning me to come abreast of him.

I keep quiet.

"You are right, of course," he says, "about being ashamed of not having done anything to bring about our liberation. We didn't earn it ourselves. You are right. Our liberation is a gift, so to speak, and not something that we have fought for and won. That bothers me, too, son. And perhaps that's why most of us, the grown-ups, are confused and bewildered and feel at a loss. We've been too preoccupied with our survival, our individual survivals, to be exact, to even think of such an eventuality as our liberation and independence. Do you understand me?"

"I think so, sir."

"You have to understand it this way, son. My father's generation was ineffective and disorganized—not only aimless but also very stupid in many ways, although the royal dynasty had more to be blamed for than anyone else in the country. They let the country get kicked around and, finally, sold down the river, you might say. Then, they handed it over to my generation and said, 'Look, we are sorry about this, but there wasn't anything we could do to save the country.'

Now, what could my generation do? We put up resistance in the beginning, to no avail of course, and we kept it up until I, for one, realized that our country's destiny was completely in the hands of all those powerful foreign countries. We couldn't bring off our liberation and independence by ourselves. Do you understand that?"

"Yes, sir. Power politics," I say, "and spheres of influence, and so forth."

"My father's generation had it in their power and will to set the country straight and do something about the declining fortune of the nation before it was too late. They could have done something, you know. They could have, on their own, brought about many necessary reforms in the country before everything was out of hand and the country was degenerating. They could have stayed wide awake and not let the country become a pawn of its powerful neighbors. They could have avoided relying too much on the foreign countries to save the nation from this and from that. The royal family was too far removed from the common people, and it was quite corrupt and its officials degenerate and rotten, and I grant that there wasn't much the common people, like your grandfather, could do, but still . . . Anyway, when it came to my generation, it was too late. The Japanese had taken over the country and their control was too entrenched and too strong to resist, but, above anything else, by then, the so-called international political pattern had come to accept Japan's occupation of our country as an established fact—already historical, you might say. Sure, we had some people abroad carrying on the independence movement, and so forth, but they accomplished very little for the people inside the country. Those of us who had to stay in the country and carry on . . . well, we could do very little, too, except, perhaps, as your grandfather said in his prayer, to sustain our faith and remain strong in spirit, hoping, just hoping, that, someday, a day like today would come. Survival, yes, that's it. Survival. Stay alive. Raise families, our children, like you, for the future. Survival, son, that's what my generation has accomplished, if that can be called an accomplishment."

We can now see our house, and I see smoke rising from the chimney. I think of my grandmother cooking in the kitchen, and I think of the wrinkled, anguished faces of the old people. I look at my father, at his pale, emaciated face, the face already wrinkled and aged, though he is only in his late thirties . . .

"You don't have to apologize to my generation, Father," I say. "You have done the best you could. We are all in it together, aren't we, Father? We share everything in our history, don't we, Father? That's our destiny as people, isn't it, sir?"

He looks at me for a long moment as we dismount outside the east gate. "I am only hoping that your generation will have enough will and strength to make sure the country will not make the same mistakes and repeat its shameful history. I only hope, son, that mere survival will not become the only goal of your generation's lives. There must be more in life than just that."

With the gravity of the situation and of the tone of his voice overwhelming me, aware so painfully that he is a man who, only several hours before, stood at the threshold of death, I pronounce with all the seriousness I can muster, "We will be all right, Father. We are going to be different from your generation, stronger and more confident. I mean, sir, my generation is beginning with our liberation and freedom, which your generation didn't have. That ought to make all the difference."

"I am sure you will be all right," he says in a tone so quiet and somber that I am at a loss to know if he is pleased with my confidence or if he is—a little sad with himself.

"I am proud of you, Father, for what you have been and for what you are now," I say, going up to him. "You've brought me out into the world and raised me the best way

you could. We will be working together, won't we, Father?
No one can really say your generation was bad and his
generation is better, can he, sir? We are all in the making of
history together, aren't we, sir?"

He nods, putting his arms around my shoulders. "Come
on," he says, "we have lots of work to do, and we will work
together, won't we?"

I press myself close to him. "You've got to get some
nourishment and improve your health. You are too thin."

"You, too," he says. "We will be all right."

"We are not going to cry anymore, are we, Father?"

"No. With a young man like you by my side? No!" And he
laughs aloud—for the first time since he came home from the
detention camp.

*   *   *

Our house has become the temporary headquarters of the
committee for self-rule and public safety. The night has
fallen. The sky is deep blue, with stars shining and the big,
bright moon rising through the clouds. A small bonfire is
burning in the middle of our courtyard. People are coming
and going. My grandmother is working in the kitchen;
the maids are running in and out of the kitchen, bringing out
dishes of food to the wooden tables by the bonfire. Wine
bottles are piled on the tables, too, and people help themselves as they rush about.

Several young men are out by the gates to watch for the
police. We now have more weapons: several hunting rifles
and enough dynamite sticks to blow up the police station if
we have to. The take-over plan is working out smoothly:
The railway station has been occupied without a fight—
the Japanese station master and his deputy have already fled
to the south, presumably to Seoul; the fire station is under
our control; the water depot and the electric transformer
station are in our hands, too. Most of the Japanese civilians,

except for those who have already taken refuge inside the police station, are now at the school auditorium, and the search through their houses has yielded weapons, mostly swords of all sizes, a few pistols, and half a dozen shotguns. A group of young men has been armed with these weapons; three young men who were home on leave from the army—those "volunteer soldiers"—have come forward and are instructing the other young men on how to use the captured weapons. They are organized into a self-defense company. A huge crowd is gathering at the open-air market place, where a gigantic bonfire is lighting up the night sky. Our neighbors are bringing food to our house to add to our stockpile of rations for those on duty here and there. A system of runners has been devised, and messages, reports, and, also, food are carried all over the town.

My father and several men of the committee are in the courtyard, huddled together over a map of the town (spread on a table by the bonfire), going over the sites where barricades and roadblocks have been set up. The roads leading into and out of the town have been sealed off, and checkpoints have been set up and manned by detachments of the self-defense company.

My father is saying, "Time to take action."

A Korean detective had come to our house from the police station with the police chief's message: The chief would like to see my father at the station. My father had sent the detective back to the chief with his message: The chief will disarm the police and turn over the station, or else the station's safety will not be guaranteed. The police chief knows that the 200 or so Japanese civilians, both those from the town and those collected from the neighboring villages, are being kept in the school's auditorium. The chief sends back another message: The police will wait for the occupation army—the Russians—to whom they will turn over the station. My father demands an immediate take-over by the town. He has given the chief one hour to make up his mind.

The committee is considering my suggestion: to threaten to burn down the station and let the police know that we are now fully armed.

My father is looking at his watch. "If they don't accept our ultimatum," he is saying, "we'll have to smoke them out."

The young man in charge of the self-defense company says, "In that case, sir, we will use our trucks to ram through the station and fight it out."

A young man is coming into the courtyard with three rifles. "We found more of these," he is saying to everyone.

The commander of the self-defense company says, "We will have plenty of ammunition and dynamite sticks to blow up the station if you give us a go-ahead."

"Let's wait a little longer," says my father.

My grandfather is putting more logs on the bonfire. Sparks fly and shoot up into the darkness. The air is chilly. My grandmother is telling everyone to eat the food on the tables.

A young man with a shotgun is running into the house from the west gate, shouting, "A man from the police is coming, sir!"

My father says, "Bring him in."

It is a Japanese police sergeant. He salutes my father and the others. He is still in his khaki uniform, but he is unarmed.

"The chief will meet with you and your people at the station gate," he says. "We agree to turn the station over to you and your committee, provided you guarantee the safety of all the Japanese subjects in town and issue safe-conducts for those who want to leave the town."

"What about the weapons?" says my father.

"We will turn them over to you, provided you issue us your receipt."

Someone laughs at the word "receipt."

"We accept your terms," says my father. "You may go."

"Sir?" the sergeant says, looking about him: young men armed with hunting rifles, shotguns, swords; boxes of dynamite sticks; several archers, mostly old people, with bows and arrows. . . .

"Yes?"

"I need an escort back to the station."

The commander of the self-defense company says to my father in Korean, "Let's keep him here, sir."

"Take him back to the station. We don't need him."

"We've got all those civilians," says a committee member.

The sergeant is led out of the courtyard.

When he is out of sight, everyone starts talking. Some urge caution. Some think we may be tricked into a trap.

"I don't think they will risk a fight," says my father. "Let's go."

My father issues a series of instructions to the commander of the self-defense company. He wants the main gate of the police station covered by those with rifles; those with the dynamite sticks should be positioned at the rear gate; more men should be deployed behind the station, just in case the police decide to break out of it; the archers, with dynamite sticks attached to their arrows, should be positioned where they can see the buildings within the grounds of the station. "Let's have a torch parade," he adds. "Tell the crowd to carry torches and surround the station, moving around and around."

Everyone rushes about. The rifles, shotguns, and pistols are checked. I snap a magazine into my pistol.

My father says to my grandfather, "We are going now. Don't worry. We'll be in touch. Keep the gates closed. I'll leave some men behind."

"We can take care of ourselves," says my grandfather.

"Where do you think you are going!" says my grandmother to me. "You are not going anywhere."

I ignore her.

"He can come with me," says my father.

"Father needs a bodyguard," I say, running out of the courtyard.

Outside the west gate, a squad from the self-defense company joins my father and the committee members. I walk beside my father, gripping the automatic. The armed men flank us, and two men go ahead. The moon is rising fast in the sky. The road is lit palely by the moonlight. Dark shadows walk before us. The streets are jammed with people, silently watching us. I hear someone behind us shout, "They are going to take over the police station!"

At the open-air market place, which is filled with several hundred people illuminated by an enormous bonfire in the center, we hear cries of "They are coming! They are coming!"

People make way for our group. They are already busy making torches. The members of the self-defense company are organizing the crowd. My father assigns a member of the committee to take charge of the crowd. We pause in the midst of all the people.

"We are going to take over the police station!" shouts my father. "And we need your help, from all of you! Are you with us?"

A roaring cheer greets him. Torches are waving. "We want you all to be calm and follow the instructions. We have weapons; we can fight the police if they want to fight us, but we don't want to see anyone get hurt. So I need your promise to obey the instructions and follow the orders. Do I have your promise? Let's go!"

The sky is lit up by hundreds and hundreds of blazing torches. A long line of people follows us toward the police station. My father wants gongs, drums, and cymbals but no singing or chanting or even shouting. "And no shooting, unless we are fired on!"

All along the way, more people are coming out of their houses, pouring out of the dark alleys. Soon, gongs and drums are being beaten, first the gong's metallic Clang-Clang, fol-

lowed by the drums' deep Boom-Boom and then the cymbals'
ear-splitting jangling. . . . Thousands of footsteps behind us
stir up the night air. The flaming sea of torches crackling
and hissing. A block before the police station, we stop. A final
conference and check: deployments of armed men, positions
of men with dynamite sticks; a signal system; procedure for
take-over . . . We move on.

At the intersection where the long stone wall of the
police station begins, the torch-bearing crowd divides—one
wave going around behind the station and the other following our group to the front of the station. The men of the
self-defense company run ahead of us, crouching, taking
positions here and there with rifles, shotguns, and dynamite
sticks. The archers are moving up the small hill by the Presbyterian church, where they will have a commanding view
of the entire police station. We go down a hilly road toward
the new main gate of the station. What used to be a sharp
climb to the station has been turned into a long, steep flight
of stone steps with a platform-like clearing halfway up. The
small plaza at the foot of the steps is quickly filled with the
crowd, with its fire-breathing torches.

The shrill, jangling cymbals, the clanging gongs, and the
rolling drums are tearing and thrashing at the dark air,
which is shredded with showers of red, orange, and white
sparks from the torches.

We pause in the middle of the plaza, waiting for word
from our runners that all our men are deployed and ready.
It comes.

Up above the long steps, half in shadows and half in the
light of the moon and the torches, the police station is silent,
and its windows are dark. We have had the electricity to
the station cut off.

My father looks at his watch.

"Now!" he says.

In a moment, the lights are on inside the station. Two
round lamps on the gates are lit. Our system of runners is

functioning efficiently. Our men have just switched the electricity for the police station back on.

We wait.

The iron gate is being opened from within. Creaks and clangs—and our armed men spring into action. They run to the foot of the stone steps, fling themselves down flat, aiming their rifles at the gate.

A man emerges from the open gate.

The commander of the self-defense company shouts upward to the station. "If there's any shooting from inside the station, we'll blow you up with dynamite!"

"There won't be any shooting!" a voice shouts down from behind the gate.

A policeman in uniform, wearing a long saber, comes down the steps, taking one step at a time, and stands erect on the flat clearing, which is halfway down.

"I am the chief of police, sir," he says.

It is suddenly hushed everywhere. Only the torches blazing and crackling and hissing. Red fires and black and smoky shadows clash and wrestle around us. I pull my automatic out of my pocket.

"Put that away," says my father quietly, looking up at the chief of police but speaking to me. "You stay here."

"I am coming with you, sir."

"I have to do this alone. You stay here with the others."

With that command, my father moves out of our circle and begins to mount the steps.

Slowly, slowly, he goes up, emerging from the slanting, dark shadows into the red fire and moonlight. His shadow trails him.

Quietly, I move away from the people and the burning fires of the torches, into the shadow of a monument in the center of the plaza; it is a statue of a soldier on a horse. There, in the shadow, still with a full view of the long steps and the gate of the station, I take out my automatic, rest it on the stone hoof of the horse on the marble pedestal, remove the safety catch, and aim the pistol at the dim figure of the chief of police.

My father takes one last step and stands by the chief of police. The chief of police salutes my father, who stands still.

We watch, holding our breath. I am flat against the cold marble of the pedestal, gripping the butt of the automatic.

I hear, somewhere in the distance, the muffled thunder of drums.

The plaza is aflame with all those torches. The air is roaring over us. No gong, no cymbal, no drum here.

Silence.

I feel my heart pounding against the marble. I place the barrel of the automatic on my elbow, squinting my eye, keeping the figure of the chief of police in the gunsight.

I see my father slowly turn toward us, then back to face the chief of police.

Abruptly, jerking out of my gunsight, the chief of police pulls himself up, saluting my father, who gives him a slight bow.

I take my eye off the gunsight and stare upward.

The chief of police removes his gleaming saber and hands it over to my father, who takes it in his left hand.

My father turns again, and the chief of police, too. They stand side by side, facing us down below.

"Everyone! Everyone!" says my father. "I have now taken over the police station in behalf of our town!"

There is silence in the plaza. No one stirs.

"I have also taken over all the public offices and facilities and the properties of the Japanese Empire in our town," my father is saying. "In behalf of the committee for self-rule and public safety, I now declare our town liberated!"

Another moment of silence; then, someone strikes a drum, and, with the BOOM-BOOM, comes a dizzying pandemonium—deafening cheers and roaring shouts and wild cries, gongs crashing, cymbals jangling, drums rolling and torches waving, the whole world tumbling and shaking and exploding. And I am running up the steps toward my father . . . and the other committee members and the men of the self-defense company and, then, the crowd, too, all running . . . I dash up to my father, who is now alone and, after throwing myself into his arms, cling to him, speechless, overcome. He pulls me to him and gives me the police chief's long saber. I am standing by him, holding up the silvery saber in my hand, watching the people surging up toward us. I clutch at my father's hand and I feel his body trembling. I look up. In the bright moonlight that bathes his face, I see tears shining in his eyes. I grip his hand and I, too, am trembling. I can't control the violent shaking. There is a light tap on my shoulder, and my father, looking into my eyes, says, "It's all right. It's over." Without a word, I nod my head, feeling the tremor within me subsiding. He says quietly, "It is your world now." I put my arm around him.

A wall of people follows us as we move up the remainder of the stone steps into the police station . . . and I remember I left my pistol on the marble pedestal of the monument of the soldier.

As we march up, drums are thundering.

Today, this night, the town is at last OURS. Today, this night, I join the ranks of men in the making of history—together.

1932–1945